NOCON

ON PHOTOGRAPHY

NOCON

ON PHOTOGRAPHY

GENE NOCON ON ASSIGNMENT
WITH EIGHT TOP PHOTOGRAPHERS

GENE NOCON
with Jonathan Glancey

THAMES MACDONALD

To Liz, Summer and Olivia — with love

A THAMES MACDONALD BOOK

© Thames Macdonald 1988

First published in Great Britain in 1988
by Macdonald & Co (Publishers) Ltd
London and Sydney

a member of Maxwell Pergamon
Publishing Corporation plc

British Library Cataloguing in Publication Data
Nocon, Gene
    Nocon on photography
    1. Photography. Techniques – Case studies
    I. Title II. Glancey, Jonathan
    770′ .28

ISBN 0-356-17532-4

Typeset by Bookworm, Salford
Printed and bound in Great Britain by
Purnell Book Production Ltd , Paulton, Bristol

Editorial Direction: Joanna Lorenz
Art Director: Linda Cole
Designer: Muffy Dodson
Picture Co-ordinator: Sharon Hutton

Macdonald & Co (Publishers) Ltd
Greater London House
Hampstead Road
London NW1 7QX

CONTENTS

Gene Nocon

INTRODUCTION

The year 1989 will mark the 150th anniversary of the invention of photography. My own involvement has been only one tenth of that, yet over the past fifteen years I have been fortunate to have met and worked with individuals recognised as the leading exponents in this field. I attribute that to my professional capacity as a photographic printer: my role has been to create and produce prints for these individuals. And over the years I have produced thousands upon thousands of prints, not only for those photographers living, but also for those no longer alive but whose life and photographic skills are embodied in the negatives they have left behind.

I've always enjoyed printing. The excitement of creating an image on a blank sheet of photo-sensitive material is for me photography. The picture-taking is but a means to the darkroom where the magic and fascination of photography can be seen.

But, away from the darkroom I found myself confused over some issues related to photography. It all came to a head at a photographic exhibition where I heard people around me talking about the picture I was standing in front of. I stared at the photograph but quite honestly could not see what they were talking about. I felt like the boy in the children's story of the emperor's new clothes who had not been told that the emperor's new suit was visible to wise men but invisible to fools. But unlike the boy who dared to point out that the emperor was in fact naked, I turned instead to the 'tailors', the photographers and experts in the field who helped shape and fashion the 'emperor's clothes', to describe to me what photography is.

How do you judge whether a photograph is good or not? Is photography an art like music and painting? How valuable is a photograph? How much hype surrounds modern photography? These are some of the questions that I set out to answer when I was invited to make a series of documentary films with Thames Television looking at the world of photography. It is not, by any means, meant to be the final word on the subject. In celebration of the 150th anniversary of photography *Life* magazine published a special issue of their journal. In the feature section entitled 'The Power of Pictures' were the words 'we invented the camera and suddenly it became possible to see inside another's mind ...' Perhaps these words best describe the very essence of photography.

This book, as well as the television series, will I hope give you further insight into the nature of photography. I also hope that you will be as fascinated as I am by the working lives of the photographers I have talked to in the preparation of this book.

HRH the Duke of York, Prince Andrew, is perhaps one of the best known amateur photographers in the public eye. I have been privileged to act as his adviser on photography over the past few years and have watched his work develop over the period. Because of his keen interest in the subject and his special position in society I hope that Prince Andrew will encourage other amateurs and newcomers to further their interest in photography. Of course, he is in the fortunate position of knowing that his photographs already have a special interest for future historians. As the one photographer able to take informal photographs of the Royal Family his collection of negatives is already priceless.

Heather Angel will show you how to take proper photographs of animals and wildlife, putting an end to those well-meant photographs that never quite come off. Richard Young and Terry O'Neill demonstrate the importance of coming in close to your subject. If you want to take memorable portraits you must never be frightened to fill the frame with your subject. In fact all the photographers I talked to have some hints that you might find useful. But I also hope that this book will encourage you to look further at the work of some of the best professional photographers. It might also start you off on a career as a collector.

At Sotheby's I was told that the highest price yet paid for a photograph in the British auction rooms was twenty thousand pounds. This was for an original print of the famous shot of the Victorian engineer Isambard Kingdom Brunel, standing against the launching chains of his great steamship *The Leviathan* (later *The Great Eastern*). Yet, another print from the same plate was expected to fetch only three thousand pounds in a recent auction. This print was simply not of the same quality, which reminds me to suggest that if you are serious about photography you should use professional printers and colour laboratories to get the best from your work. Very often your negatives could be much better than is apparent from the prints you pick up, sometimes disappointed, in the high street. High-speed processes and plastic 'paper' can never match the crafted work of professionals. Too often colours are washed out and prints do not have the clarity you should expect of your camera lens.

But whatever your own personal conclusions, the main thing is that you like some of the work shown, see how professionals go about their business and pick up a camera with a fresh eye. Who knows – one of your pictures might end up in the National Portrait Gallery.

BIRTHDAY FLOWERS *by Gene Nocon. This picture epitomises for me what photography is all about: namely the study, or capture, of light. For me, this image was a happy accident – lighting up a bunch of flowers given to my wife, they became transfused with glory. The skill of the photographer, to my mind, is the ability to analyse and re-create this effect in the studio, and to recognise and capture it when it occurs naturally.*

CHAPTER ONE

THE PRESS AND THE COMMISSIONED

THE CELEBRITY PHOTOGRAPHERS: THE 'UNINVITED'
RICHARD YOUNG AND THE 'INVITED' TERRY O'NEILL.

Newspaper readers seem pretty star-struck. The demand for candid photographs of celebrities continues to grow as the stars themselves protest increasingly over the guerilla tactics of the paparazzi. Of course, many celebrities and celebrity photographers feed willingly on one another. No film or rock star, newsworthy royal, actor of the moment or fame-seeking starlet would eat dinner at Langan's, drink at Harry's Bar or dance at Annabel's if they really wanted to avoid publicity. In fact, as Peter Stringfellow told me, 'celebs' or rising stars deliberately choose to spend an evening in restaurants and nightclubs famed for their marauding packs of paparazzi when they have a new film, book or album in need of a little promotion.

Richard Young, 'Prince of the Paparazzi', is much in demand by celebrities and even invited to private parties. Clearly, despite the howls of outrage, there are plenty of stars looking forward to the next morning's gossip columns. Terry O'Neill also began his career as a photo-journalist, though of a different kind, capturing the excitement of big stories rather than stars caught unawares. Today he is one of the most sought-after celebrity portrait photographers.

I spent a hectic night out with Richard Young in his daily quest for people and pictures that the *Daily Express* could use in their Diary page the next morning. In contrast I joined Terry O'Neill on a more formal, yet necessarily hurried session, on the set of the new television film 'The Ripper' starring Michael Caine and Jane Seymour. Michael and Jane gave me some very sane views on the paparazzi. What I learnt, as you can read, is that photographers and stars are partners in an incestuous, if sometimes tempestuous, relationship.

The name paparazzi was in fact adopted from Federico Fellini's feted film 'La Dolce Vita', released in 1960. Set in a decadent and star-gazing Rome, one character that kept popping up was a photographer called Paparazzo, doing what today's paparazzi do − crowding the stars. But if Fellini gave the role both glamour and a name, he did not create the phenomenon.

Richard Young is known as the Prince of the Paparazzi. A friend of many celebrities, he is often invited by them to record private events. Most of his work appears in the Diary column of the *Daily Express,* although his first pictures appeared in the *Evening Standard* when he was working as an assistant in a bookshop. That was fourteen years ago. In those early days Richard admits that he was 'pretty wild'. He got his best pictures and the ones that other photographers missed by shinning up drainpipes, climbing through windows and gate-crashing parties.

Richard stumbled into photography very much by accident. In 1974 a journalist friend of his set up a secret interview for *Rolling Stone* magazine in London with John Paul Getty junior, only weeks after Getty's release from kidnappers who cut off one of his ears. Richard who had been trying (unsuccessfully, he claims) to take some landscape pictures for his boss at the bookshop was invited along to take some personal photographs. He was advised to take the roll of film along to Fleet Street and dropped into the offices of the *Evening Standard* who published the pictures the next day. Richard was delighted to see his by-line and to receive a cheque for thirty pounds.

The *Evening Standard* asked him to produce more pictures and packed him off to Richard Burton's fiftieth birthday party (November 1975), a private event at the Dorchester. The lobby was packed with newshounds and paparazzi. With all the ingenuousness and effrontery of the newcomer, Richard simply walked through a glass door following a member of the hotel staff and found himself in the ballroom. He confided in the DJ who left him to spin the records while he went off for a break. So while Richard Burton and Elizabeth Taylor were kissing and cutting a huge cake, Richard was acting as disc jockey a few feet away with a camera under his jacket. He managed to fire off about half a dozen photographs before Miss Taylor became a little suspicious and asked him politely, but firmly, to stop. Perhaps he was a family friend; nobody seemed to know – no-one knew him as a member of the Fleet Street pack. Richard made his excuses and left, securing his name that evening as a photographer who came up with the goods when no-one else could.

Fourteen years into his career as a paparazzo, Richard is still leader of the pack. Yet, despite his fearsome reputation, he is trusted by many celebrities. Recently he was invited by George and Olivia Harrison to photograph them at home in Henley. He was acting purely as a family photographer and would not even consider selling the pictures to a newspaper.

ELIZABETH TAYLOR *clearly taken aback at the door of the Dorchester Hotel. Miss Taylor had just returned from an Eric Clapton concert and was in no mood for pleasantries, although she and Richard Young jog along in what Richard describes as a love-hate relationship. Taken as with most Young shots on Tri-X with a Leica M6.*

ANNIE LENNOX AND DAVE STEWART *of the Eurythmics, two of the music celebrities attending the annual Ivor Novello Awards at the Grosvenor House Hotel. This is one of the functions to which Richard is*

Terry O'Neill was one of *the* pop photographers of the Swinging Sixties. As a very young and recently recognised celebrity photographer he was recording his own generation as they burst into stardom. Terry was a part of their success and unsurprisingly he is a close friend of many of the established stars in the music world.

Yet Terry never intended to be a photographer. He began his career as a jazz musician. Back in 1959 he tried to get a job as an air steward with BOAC in the vain hope that this would give him the chance of playing on both sides of the Atlantic. In fact BOAC offered him a job as a trainee in its technical photography department. Terry learnt the basics of his craft photographing bits of wrecked planes. Sent on a day-release art school course, Terry went on photo-reportage assignments. These led to his big break.

One day prowling around Heathrow he took a picture of a plump, middle-aged man dressed in a 'beautiful suit', fast asleep. That man was 'Rab' Butler, then foreign secretary and tipped to succeed Harold Macmillan as Prime Minister. A journalist watching the twenty-year-old O'Neill told him to send the film to the *Sunday Despatch*. They published what became a classic press photograph. Sadly, Terry forgot to save the negative.

On the strength of this, Terry was offered a job on the *Daily Sketch*, which was keen to attract young readers. Sent out to photograph the Beatles and the Rolling Stones at the very start of their recording careers, Terry was able to match his musical interests with his flair for photography. He was able to decide which singers or groups were going to make it and cover them appropriately. Elton John was one of his finds. He has been invited to cover the singer's major tours ever since.

In the seventies Terry began photographing sporting heroes. His approach took sports photography off the back pages of newspapers and into the centre sections and eventually the covers of the colour supplements. In recent years Terry has been developing his photography in other directions. He is much in demand on film sets, for example, although this has given him some of the relatively few professional headaches he has suffered. 'The worst subject I ever had was Robert Redford. He is so nice, yet so painfully shy that after three unsuccessful rolls I just had to give up. It was that painful. Some people are just too shy to relate to a still camera.'

GROUP PORTRAIT OF THE HORROR
STARS. *This photograph was taken on location
for the 'House of Long Shadows', in
Hampshire, England 1983. Back row,
Christopher Lee and Vincent Price; front
row John Carradine and Peter Cushing.
Terry O'Neill photographs actors both in*

THE MOST STYLISH PART OF SATURDAY

dx

WITH THE DAILY EXPRESS

ISSUE THREE MAY 21 1988

Jerr
Hall

Fashioned
in heaven

Spotting
the Ball:
Essential
Summer
Frolics

Positively
stately:
The rocking
acres of
Knebworth

PORTRAIT OF SARAH FERGUSON *as
dashing and mysterious pilot. Terry was
particularly pleased with this 6 x 6 colour
transparency which captures the Duchess of
York in a studiously casual manner. It was
difficult to imagine taking photographs like
this of the Royal Family until very recently.*

'THE PRINCE OF THE PAPARAZZI'

The paparazzi are those photographers who pop up unexpectedly with flashguns at grand social occasions or private parties hosted by stars of stage and screen. They are often portrayed as vultures with cameras clutched to their claws. But is this a fair picture? I accompanied Richard Young one night to find out.

A night out on the town with Richard Young is a hair-raising experience, not least because it entails hanging on to the back of one of his two Harley-Davidson motorbikes as he shuttles between San Lorenzo's, Harry's Bar, Langan's Brasserie and Stringfellows. Richard wastes no time. Pulling up outside Harry's Bar he does a once around the block looking for cars he recognises. Absence of chauffeur-driven limos is a sure sign of a quiet night. Richard hurries on in pursuit of his goal, a candid celebrity picture for tomorrow's *Daily Express*.

Our night out begins in the Art Deco offices of the *Daily Express,* one of the last newspapers still in Fleet Street. We met Ross Benson, editor of the *Express* Diary and Terry Evans, the paper's Deputy Picture Editor. Although he has many of his own contacts, Richard must talk to Ross about which celebrities are known to be in town and about the newspaper's interest in them. A short, staccato discussion between Ross and Richard is almost chilling. You quickly learn which celebrities are in and which ones are out. 'No more on Khashoggi', snaps Ross; 'don't want Susannah Constantine. Victor Lowndes? Party for twenty-five ex-Bunny girls? OK, take a look at that'.

'A LOT OF PEOPLE LIKE SEEING PICTURES OF A FILM STAR OR PAGE THREE GIRL OUT WITH SOME ROCK STAR. NO-ONE'S GETTING HURT . . .'

With Richard and Ross agreed on what should be covered, we look through last night's results with Terry Evans. Terry cannot find what he wants. What happened to Jerry Hall and Mick Jagger? 'They're in Ireland. They might be back today.' 'I'll tell the airport man to keep a watch', says Evans. Celebrities, I learn, are part of a fairly fixed circus troupe. The papers and their readers' interest in Mick Jagger and Jerry Hall, Rod Stewart and Elizabeth Taylor never seems to diminish.

Ross Benson is looking for pictures that capture celebrities with the new man or woman in their life, at major events and in embarrassing positions. One of his favourite Young pictures was one of the restaurateur Peter Langan asleep under one of the tables in his famous brasserie after a heavy working lunch. 'We captioned that something like "Peter Langan entertaining fellow diners at lunchtime."'

Richard and I roar off into the night. Our first port of call is San Lorenzo's, the Fulham restaurant favoured by young professionals. Richard parks his bike out of sight as it has become well known, a certain sign that out there beyond the intimacy of the restaurant walls a paparazzo lies in wait. Richard checks the cars parked outside, makes a snap decision that there is no-one worth photographing inside, and powers us down to Harry's Bar. Again no luck. This, as Ross Benson said, is not an easy way to make a living.

Now it is onwards to Langan's. Richard says that one of the rules of engagement between star and photographer is 'never to photograph people eating in a restaurant'. You find out who's there and capture them like butterflies in a net as they leave. Unlike some paparazzi, Richard is prepared to fork out for the occasional meal in a restaurant like Langan's; he reasons that trade must be a two-way business. If you

are living off the back of establishments like Peter Langan's famous brasserie, then you have to support the place like any other regular. This, I found, also makes Richard more popular with staff who are likely to give him tip-offs as to who is dining with whom that week and at which tables they will be sitting. In fact as our evening progresses I discover that doormen, waiters, waitresses and taxi drivers are some of Richard's most important assistants.

At Langan's the man keenest to be photographed is the proprietor, so we make our excuses and head off for Stringfellows. While Richard hunted, I talked to Peter Stringfellow who said that he has banned the paparazzi and now employs a full-time in-house photographer called Margot instead. 'Sometimes we have had six or seven photographers in here, which was getting a bit silly. Still, I don't think paparazzi are destructive. I don't think they can kill off someone unless that person is on a course to self destruct anyway.'

'STANDING OUTSIDE A RESTAURANT IN THE MIDDLE OF WINTER, JUST ON THE OFF-CHANCE THAT SOMEONE FAMOUS MAY COME OUT — IT'S NOT AN EASY WAY TO MAKE A LIVING.'

Steve Strange was sitting next to Peter. What did he think of the paparazzi? 'There were quite a few of them who helped me to build my career. You have to take it. If you become classed as a celebrity then you know that they're going to follow you. It's a position you put yourself in.' Bill Buckley, sitting next to Steve Strange, found himself famous for little more than Andy Warhol's statutory fifteen minutes. 'One moment they were surrounding me. Then one day I walked into the BBC where I was working at the time and there was no-one there. I asked the receptionist what had happened and she said, 'Oh, you're over now. There's a fresh rumour that Debbie Rix and Selina Scott have fallen out over Breakfast Time. You're yesterday's news.' 'And, after all', smiles Bill ruefully, 'today's news is really just tomorrow's fish and chip paper.'

Richard then roars back to Fleet Street via Langan's. He has been tipped off that Dolph Lundgren is eating there with a girlfriend, and if he hurries he should catch them coming out of the

Dolph Lundgren, the Swedish star of science fiction and fantasy films, outside Langan's with his girlfriend. Peter Langan's brasserie is one of the gathering places of celebrities and a location that Richard never fails to visit on his motorbike jaunts through night-time London.

Richard Young (top), draped in Nikons, talks to actor Lance Percival at the Royal Berkshire Polo Club. Richard enjoys an easy rapport with most of the celebrities he photographs. Below: You cannot always be sure just who is a celebrity and who just captures your lens. Just in case Richard snapped this couple.

door. Richard does get the picture and it appears the next morning in the *Daily Express.* So, after a night of tearing around expending a lot of energy, if little film, Richard has succeeded in getting the one picture his Diary editor wants to publish. It has been a successful night on the town.

'THE PICTURE EDITORS BECOME MORE AND MORE BLASÉ, AND SO THE PHOTOGRAPHS HAVE TO BECOME EVEN WILDER AS A RESULT.'

I also joined Richard at the Mayfair Ladies' Day Match at the Royal Berkshire Polo Club at Winkfield Row. On that occasion, where so many faces were crammed across a wide area, Richard

brought his new fully automatic Nikon 801 with a selection of telephoto lenses. Richard finds the camera a godsend, but chooses not to use the auto-focus. He needs to select faces very carefully and needs to control the focus without the camera overriding his choice. During the polo match Richard much prefers keeping his distance behind a 300 or 400mm lens. 'If I went up to people and said can I take a photograph of you, nine times out of ten they would say yes, but the shot would be posed and never as interesting as the spontaneous situations I can see from afar.' So we found a nest location and sniped from the side of the field. The polo match is like a picnic for Richard after a week chasing round late-night London.

In the nightclubs, bars and receptions Richard carries at least a brace of compact Leica M6 cameras. These might cost fifteen hundred pounds each, but in Richard's hands they work very hard for their living. They slip unseen into his pockets. 'When I do pop them out, a lot of people say "Oh, it's just a little camera", but it will take the pictures that will appear in the Ross Benson column the next morning.'

Below: Pamela Stephenson is a full-time celebrity. Her provocative behaviour and colourful outfits are copy fodder for newspaper diary columnists.

Left: Richard and me with actress Stephanie Powers at Winkworth Row. Richard normally carries three cameras on an assignment. On occasions such as this he has the autofocus control cut out. The problem with it, he thinks, is that you are effectively unable to home in on a single face in a crowd. Richard needs precise control.

A scenic shot of one of the polo games in action on Ladies' Day at the Royal Berkshire. A typical English summer's day.

TERRY O'NEILL AT THE FILM SET

Terry O'Neill is, like Richard Young, one of the best-known star hunters in Britain – but with one major difference. Terry works solely on commission, photographing celebrities for magazines and private portraits. I went with him on location to the set of a new television film, screened in October 1988.

Terry had been commissioned to photograph Michael Caine and Jane Seymour, stars of the new television film 'The Ripper' planned to coincide with the one-hundredth anniversary of the grisly and mysterious Ripper murders. The photographs were used this autumn for publicity purposes. Terry needed to capture images that could be used on both small-scale brochures and giant advertising hoardings, some up to twenty feet across. The photo-session took place on the film set at the old Holloway Sanatorium, a terrifying Victorian building which is where the great *Ballet Russe* dancer Nijinsky was locked away during the years of his madness. The building, not surprisingly, is said to be haunted.

The day's assignment would be difficult simply because Terry would have so little time. As filming was in progress, a hugely expensive medium, the two stars would have to dash along to sit for Terry between takes. As there was no room for manoeuvre, the important thing for Terry was to have set up ready a small indoor studio with the equipment primed for the quick photographs that would be necessary. I offered to stand in for both Michael Caine and Jane Seymour for the polaroids, while Terry put his preparations in hand.

Most of 'The Ripper' was being filmed on location in Spitalfields and down by the London docks. The old sanatorium was chosen for its atmospheric Victorian interiors. Terry was using a medium format camera for the event. This seemed a long way removed from his role as a rapid fire 35mm photographer. 'You have to use this kind of equipment now,' he explained. 'The quality demanded by magazines for front covers and by advertising agencies is much higher than it has ever been. You need the large format so that they can blow the pictures up to very large sizes.'

Terry had also brought his own lighting. This was important given the rushed nature of the job. Terry was keen to have everything well organised so that when Michael and Jane finally managed to turn up there would be no last-minute panic with the equipment. Given the fact that the actors might be called back on to the set within seconds of sitting for the photo call, it was important that they should be as relaxed as possible. It is essential for a good portrait photographer to keep the ever-increasing technology at bay so that it does not terrify the sitter.

We spent a lot of time waiting. 'This is really a high-class paparazzi act', ventured Terry. 'It's much the same thing, waiting like Richard Young sometimes has to wait. For many photographers ninety percent of their work is waiting, with something like ten seconds of super-charged time to take the pictures.'

'IT'S DIFFICULT NOT TO AVOID THE TRAP OF BEING KNOWN FOR A PARTICULAR STYLE – LIKE WHEN YOU HAVE A HIT RECORD, PEOPLE WANT THE SAME THING AGAIN AND AGAIN.'

Terry took the very first publicity photographs of Jane Seymour when she was just seventeen and played the role of Solitaire alongside Roger Moore in the James Bond film 'Live and Let Die'. Jane, according to Terry, is currently at the

Terry and me on location outside the Victorian sanatorium used as the set of The Ripper, *a new film starring Michael Caine and Jane Seymour.*

peak of her career. 'She's been on television this year from January to December. She's on everything it seems except the news and the weather.' Terry commented on Jane's beauty, explaining that it was unlike the transient beauty of a fashion model. 'You know every model says that they want to be a movie star, and by some of their looks you'd think they ought to be. But acting is not just about beauty. It comes from deep inside and you have to find that when you're photographing someone like Jane.'

Does Terry have to pose actors like models? 'No. Actors just sink into a role. There are really only a very few at the top who don't know how to project themselves at the other end of a still camera. Jane Seymour is very easy to photograph. She'll give you a variety of expressions and looks.'

Jane arrives and in the few minutes we have to capture her on film she talked about press photographers. 'Actresses are always terrified of having stills taken, but Terry makes me feel secure.'

'THE KEY THING IS TO RESPECT THE PERSON YOU'RE PHOTOGRAPHING. IT'LL SHOW IN YOUR WORK — IT'S WHAT MAKES THE PICTURE SPECIAL.'

Legend has it that it was Greta Garbo's determination to lead a very private life that set newspaper photographers after her like a pack of hungry wolves. The more the great star wanted to be alone, the more interest the papers showed in her. Jane Seymour avoids the trap. She says that she never forgets the advice that David Frost gave her at the première of the Bond film 'Live and Let Die' (1971), when she was natural bait for the paparazzi. 'He said whenever you walk in or out of a private place, always smile from ear to ear because that way they can never print a bad story about you.' The paparazzi and the newspaper picture editors still like celebrities to scowl.

Terry has to work quickly as Jane is gone almost as soon as she has arrived. He was not quite happy with the hat

Jane was wearing, but time was too pressing to rearrange everything. Terry came in very close, but explained afterwards that this type of photograph is often not what art editors want. They like a border around or on top of a picture – sky is always helpful – so that they can add in cover lines without having to crop the image. On a hurried day like this Terry has to compromise a good deal, but by coming in close he ensures a distinctive picture.

Michael Caine follows. In the film he plays a police inspector in charge of the Ripper investigation. He could even be one of the suspects and Terry wanted to get that feeling of ambiguity in his portrait. Michael has known Terry's work for a long time and feels confident in his ability. 'Terry took all those marvellous stills with me and Bob Hoskins on the set of 'Mona Lisa'.'

Michael Caine is a very relaxed subject. He is also laid-back about the

paparazzi. 'I'm not in this business for fame, but for satisfaction and money. But I know the score when it comes to newspapers and photographs.' Michael says that he manages to bore the photographers by being all too easily accessible. 'I just stand there and pose. I don't care. I've offered myself up on a plate so many times that the paparazzi have got bored and leave me alone now.' So if you want to avoid unnecessary press attention, remember to say 'Cheese'.

Above: Jane Seymour receives the attention of make-up artists on the set. Terry's portraits had to be taken in very short breaks between film takes.

RICHARD YOUNG'S PHOTOGRAPHS

Shikira Caine, wife of actor Michael Caine, at the celebrity polo tournament. Richard shoots colour film in case his editors require it, but like many professional photographers prefers to work in black and white. 'The problem with colour', he says, 'is that you have no control over the finished product.'

Pamela Stephenson again, this time in full living colour. Richard is just as puzzled as the rest of us as to who will make celebrity status. Some models and many pop 'stars' hog the headlines for a few weeks and then vanish in a flash of light bulbs. Pamela Stephenson, however, is a hardy perennial.

Bill Wyman and friend (with Kenny Jones's daughter) at Winkworth Row. Bill Wyman is used to being a celebrity in full public view. After twenty-five years as a member of the Rolling Stones he has become used to photographers recording his every action. Like many long-term rock stars he trusts Richard implicitly. Richard, in his turn, keeps a sharp check on the words that accompany his photographs in the gossip columns. A twisting of the truth could make him enemies he does not want.

TERRY O'NEILL'S PHOTOGRAPHS

*Group portrait of the Ripper suspects from
the new film. Back row: Gary Shail
(pimp), Jonathan Moore (reporter). Middle
row: Armand Assante (actor), Michael
Caine (police inspector), Lewis Collins
(police sergeant). Front row: Ken Bones
(psychic medium), Edward Judd (head of
CID, Scotland Yard), Michael Godard
(vigilante leader).*

A close-up portrait of Michael Caine and Jane Seymour, stars of the film. Michael plays Detective Inspector Abberline of Scotland Yard who heads the Ripper investigation. Jane plays Emma Prentice, a sketch artist for the London Star *newspaper. Terry has filled the frame with a tight composition that has maximum impact.*

Portrait of Kelly Cryer as Annette, a young
French prostitute who 'entertains'
gentlemen and who is recruited by the
police to help track down Jack the Ripper.
Kelly is actually one of four Whitechapel
whores who add spice to the film.

CHAPTER TWO

IMAGES THAT INFLUENCE

ALBERT WATSON ON AN ADVERTISING ASSIGNMENT IN MANHATTAN;
AN ALTERNATIVE APPROACH FROM DAVID A. BAILEY IN LONDON.

Albert Watson is one of New York's leading advertising photographers. His output is prolific and, as thousands of readers of *Vogue* will testify, of the highest calibre. I went to Manhattan to join Albert on a photo-session for Fabrice, dress designer to Elizabeth Taylor, Joan Collins, Mary Tyler Moore and many other *grandes dames* of the screen. The evening we spent on the assignment served as a sharp reminder that an advertising photographer's life is not as glamorous as has been portrayed. The real world of the photographer is certainly one of beautiful models, but like the products they are promoting, they are, for the most part, live props – part of an image that the photographer sees through the lens and records on celluloid.

The work is demanding, split-second stuff. The sheer amount of money invested in equipment, locations and models and the need to meet magazine deadlines means that a modern advertising photographer simply cannot afford to be a philandering dilettante. Only too aware of the onus on him to produce the perfect shot each time, Albert, the complete professional, has invested in a remarkable purpose-built studio, the first, in fact, that has been built from ground up specially for a photographer.

The day after the Manhattan session I joined Albert in the studio for a still-life assignment for *Vogue.* Well, not exactly still-life, as Albert planned to highlight a pair of new snakeskin shoes with a live snake. I also talked to Albert about the relationship a photographer has with the magazines and their art directors, and whether as a top professional he prefers working on editorial or advertising sessions: advertising has become more, not less, glamorous over the years and is a much more lucrative field than editorial for a photographer.

A young London photographer with an ambivalent attitude towards magazines like *Vogue* is David A. Bailey. David feels that the use of black models in such mainstream magazines is stereotyped. I went to discuss the role of black photography with David and to watch him at work on an experimental photo session in which he promised that accepted images of what black and white means would be deliberately confused.

Albert Watson has photographed more than two hundred and fifty covers for American *Vogue*. He was the official photographer at the wedding of HRH Prince Andrew and Sarah Ferguson. His work has been published worldwide. Yet, curiously, Albert Watson came to photography rather late in life. Born in Edinburgh, Watson worked for a spell in a chocolate factory before studying art and graphic design in Dundee. He went on to study film and television as a post-graduate student at the Royal College of Art. His only plans to date were to teach at art college.

But when his wife Elizabeth took up a teaching post in Los Angeles in 1970, Albert followed and began toying with photography. Through a friend he met the advertising manager of Max Factor, the cosmetic company, and talked himself – Albert is rarely lost for words – into an hour's photo session with a Max Factor model. Albert persuaded the girl to stay the whole day. On that first professional session, Albert worked from 7.30 am to 6.15 pm and ploughed his way through sixty rolls of film. Max Factor bought just two pictures, but that was enough to get Albert's career as a photographer off the ground. He was delighted when he was offered what he thought was one hundred and fifty dollars for each photograph. Calling Max Factor to double-check, the company's accounts department apologised but insisted that one thousand five hundred dollars a picture was their limit. And then they chose a third picture. 'Four and a half thousand dollars was a lot of money for a day's photography back in 1970', recalls an amused Watson. 'It still is.'

Since then Albert has not looked back. He moved from Los Angeles to New York in 1976 where his speed and professionalism have earned him both considerable respect and the money to invest in what must be the most stunning and sophisticated purpose-built photographer's studio in the world. And yet, despite the demanding nature of his profession, Albert still has time to craft some notably fine still-life photography purely for his own satisfaction. Giant blow-ups of these adorn the walls of his lower Manhattan studio.

Albert's well-known ability to work at terrific speed under pressure was also one of the reasons he was appointed official photographer at the last Royal Wedding. He was given just twelve minutes to take nine official shots at Buckingham Palace. Albert spent three twelve-hour days setting up and rehearsing. On the eve of the great day he was taking a practice photograph of the wedding group, having roped in eighteen cleaning ladies for the occasion. Perched on the top of a tall ladder peering through his Hasselblad at a gaggle of grinning Mrs Mopps, Albert was interrupted by a woman's voice enquiring as to which one was supposed to be her . It was, to Albert's great discomfort, the Queen, who was in fact quite amused by the farcical situation and spent a quarter of an hour discussing arrangements. In the end, Albert was pleased with the results. 'I think that the photography was very vibrant and that we captured some of the saturation of colour, not only of what everybody was wearing, but somehow the magic of the event.'

PAINTERLY FEATURE FOR ITALIAN
VOGUE. *Taken on a large format Hasselblad,
this transparency captures a fashion image
unusual in that the model is not wearing
the complete outfit portrayed. The point of
the picture is to portray an image of the
clothes, a typical Watson approach.*

GIRL IN HAT. *One of Albert Watson's favourite photographs. Taken in harsh midday sunlight in Naples, this black and white image demonstrates how a photographer can manipulate shadows. The model's face appears as a two-dimensional silhouette, while her shoulders stand out in three sunlit dimensions.*

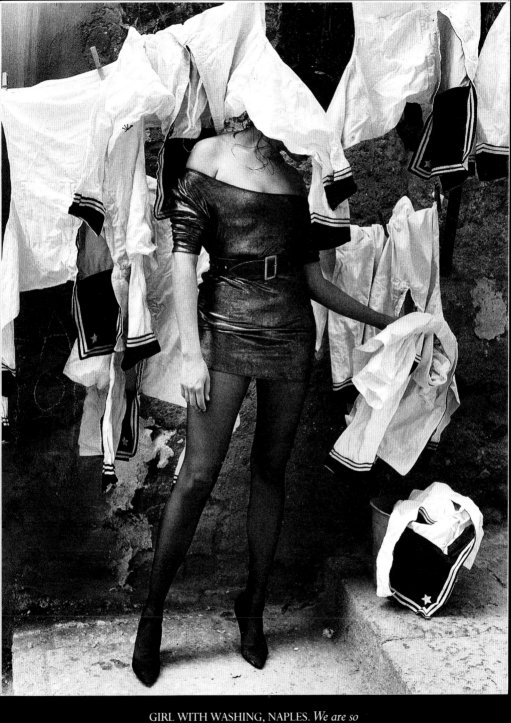

GIRL WITH WASHING, NAPLES. *We are so used to seeing the faces of models that an image like this is almost disturbing. Albert believes that this kind of treatment adds a real sense of mystery to advertising photographs. This is a clever composition,*

EMBRACING COUPLE. *A powerful black and white print contrasting the smooth complexion and sophisticated silk dress of the girl with the unshaven and workaday garb of the male model. A study in shadows and textures, this print is one of those that Albert has blown up to larger-than-life size and hung on the walls of his studio.*

ESSAY IN SURREALISM. *A natural backdrop
can take on an unreal quality in certain
lighting conditions and when, as in this
example, the model and plant appear as
intruders into the backdrop. As in many
of his best photographs, Albert has
explored the effects of contrasting light
and materials.*

ALBERT WATSON IN MANHATTAN

Who says that the world of advertising photography is a glamorous one? Of course it can be, but when you have been standing for hours with Albert Watson under New York's Brooklyn Bridge on a wet evening waiting to set up a shot for Vogue, the glamour begins to wane.

The scene is Brooklyn's famous Gothic bridge on a stormy late spring evening. Albert, his lead assistant Joseph Montezinos, model Pam Ross – Pam has featured in countless Watson pictures – dresser, make-up artist and hairdresser are all busy preparing for a publicity photograph for Fabrice while the sky gets darker. It could rain at any time. In fact for the next forty-eight hours it will pour down incessantly. Yet Albert is holding back until the moment when cleaning staff begin switching on the lights of the looming Wall Street office towers facing us across the choppy water, when it is neither light nor dark. This is the time when the red Fabrice dress, the subject of this session, will look most striking against the brooding backdrop.

The Brooklyn Bridge thunders to the sound of rush-hour traffic, police sirens wail like vixens, the Staten Island ferry passes backwards and forwards churning up the murky water, and two policemen look on. Behind us a vast illuminated sign claims that the temperature is 63 degrees Fahrenheit, although everyone looks chilled to the marrow.

'TECHNIQUE IN PHOTOGRAPHY IS OF MAJOR IMPORTANCE BUT IS NOT THE ABSOLUTE END. IT'S NOTHING IF THERE ISN'T EMOTION IN THE PHOTOGRAPH ITSELF. BUT TECHNIQUE IS A KEY THAT CAN OPEN UP MARVELS TO YOU.'

Above: Albert Watson angles the lamp he needs to light up model Pam Ross against the cloudy Wall Street skyline.

Below: The brooding early evening backdrop of Wall Street. Albert held back his photograph until the optimum point between romantic twilight and stygian gloom.

Albert is aware that any picture of a model looking windswept against a city skyline could be a stereotype. 'The problems of stereotyping affect a photographer every working day. The demands of advertising, in particular, when you are being paid well to evoke an image that your client has in the back of his or her mind, can easily lead to clichéd images. You have to be very careful.'

Albert poses Pam with her back to the camera. A peep through the viewfinder shows her melting into the dramatically charged Wall Street backdrop. 'This is how I want the shot. Pam appears as a woman in New York, not just as a model. I think it's also more romantic to see her from the back. You're automatically curious about the way she'll look when she turns round. This way the shot has a sense of mystery.'

'MAKING MONEY IS NOT A PROBLEM PROVIDED YOU REALLY KNOW WHAT YOU ARE DOING.'

Is Albert sure that this picture will best sell the product? 'Well you could choose one that looks like a shot from a catalogue, but this one should have a more magical quality about it.' Much photography in advertising is used today to capture a feeling for a product, rather than to examine that product in minute detail. People are buying a dream as much as a real garment.

But in choosing to pose Pam with her face hidden, why bother with a glamorous model? Could you use the girl next door and save three thousand dollars? 'Definitely not. You've got to have a girl who is beautiful. You never know what shot you might finally want. The best one might be looking at Pam face on. In any case you must always remember what the public is looking for in advertising photography: it's looking for fantasy, it's looking for romance. The dress by itself is only a part of the equation. You could just put it on a hanger and shoot it in the studio. You might even get a good shot. But people want to imagine themselves in this situation: it's the image of this girl, in this dress, that will sell.'

'IF I HAVE A PROBLEM IT'S BEING A WORKAHOLIC. THE ABILITY TO RELAX HELPS YOUR WORK IMMENSELY.'

The actual photography is very fast. It has to be, because the light fades quickly. Using flash and Professional Eck-tachrome film, Albert appears to race through the critical process of capturing the carefully pre-arranged image we have waited so patiently to record. We leave the Bridge while veteran film maker Gordon Willis and crew are busy using the same location to film a cinema ad for Michelob beer. As Albert has already said, stereotypes are only too easy.

Above: Model Pam Ross works regularly with Albert Watson. Here she receives the attention of the hairdresser before changing into the red Fabrice dress.

Below: Behind the scenes on location. Albert looks on patiently as Pam gets ready and the sky gets darker. This is romantic?

The next day we will see the results as the transparencies are rushed back from the colour processing laboratory. In the meantime Albert and I meet up at his studio on the corner of Washington Street and Jane Street the next morning to photograph a still-life of a new pair of snakeskin shoes for *Vogue*. Albert's studio is impressive by any standards and reflects his keen interest in modern architecture. The main studio punches up through two floors of the new building. It measures twenty-eight by seventy-five feet, is cooled by six powerful extractor fans and is brought to life through four professional loudspeakers alternately pumping out pop and opera. At one end, lit up in a small atrium, is a Carrara marble statue of an angel sculpted by the Milanese artist Antonio Angenti in the late nineteenth century. The wingless angel adds to the remarkably serene atmosphere of the studio. 'We decided to put her wings else-

where', explains Watson, 'otherwise there was the danger of the place looking too much like a funeral parlour.'

Upstairs there are changing and make-up rooms for models and every possible ancillary service needed to make a photographer's studio run smoothly. The studio, when in session, is animated by Albert who appears to run at full charge all day. Albert believes that image is all important when working in the advertising industry. 'A studio like this works for me, of course, but it also imparts confidence to people investing in me.' The hi-tech studio is a considerable investment, but Albert has played the real estate market wisely and although expensive, the four-storey building (the top two floors house Watson's apartment) has virtually paid for itself.

'THIS BUSINESS DEMANDS ABSOLUTE PROFESSIONALISM.'

Bill Perron, the herpatologist, turns up with a number of different-sized bottles. Each one provides a mobile home for the colourful, but harmless, Pueblan, Mexican and Sinaloan milk snakes (so-called because American and Mexican farmers, finding them in cow sheds, believed for a very long time that they sucked cows dry of milk). A snake is chosen and paired up with one of the fashion shoes designed by Susan Bennis and Warren Edwards. Albert uses a 150mm lens with an extension tube for the photograph. 'You can't rush a shot like this with a live animal involved. Sometimes it can take two working days to get the shot you really want. On average you might expect to get a decent image about once every two hours.'

Is the image of a snake inside a snakeskin shoe a bit obvious? 'It's certainly the most obvious thing you can do', Albert agrees. 'One of my favourite still-lives for an advertising shot is one showing a waterproof watch inside a goldfish bowl, which is about as obvious as you can get. I like simple images. Handled well they can be familiar and yet memorable at the same time.'

While preparing the set, Albert discusses the nature of working with different clients. 'Take this snake shot. I think it would work really well in black and white. In fact I love black and white photography. But the advertisers and magazines want colour and it's difficult to argue with them when they're paying. If you pay a taxi driver to take you to 57th Street, you expect him to take you straight there and nowhere else. It's much the same kind of relationship with photography and advertisers. They are paying you, as a professional, to capture an image that they already have more or less in mind.

'Working with advertisers obviously puts some limit on what a photographer can do. But it is well paid. Editorial work on the other hand is much less well paid, yet offers considerably more freedom. After discussing a shoot with the art director of a magazine, it is often a case of getting on with it in your own way. Of course the pictures can still be rejected, even your favourites.'

'I LOVE TO TAKE PHOTOGRAPHS JUST
FOR MYSELF. I JUMP AT
OPPORTUNITIES TO MAKE MY
OWN IMAGES.'

Although Albert enjoys the cut and thrust of advertising photography, he claims that he will welcome the day when his photography can become a hobby. His set-up in Manhattan does demand that Watson works hard and lucratively, yet he says that he could easily give it all up if he wanted to. 'I don't see the studio as a burden, as it is something I can give up at any time. Everything depends on how I feel about what I'm doing at any particular moment. I could drop New York and set up in London, Paris or Milan. I guess that if I went to London, I would be working much more for myself, so I wouldn't

Opposite: Watson's purpose-built Manhattan studio on the corner of Washington Street and Jane Street. Inside it is a photographer's dream come true.

Below: Albert Watson poses for my camera in the studio. On the walls and reflected in the glass-topped table are two of his non-commercial still-lives.

need a studio quite like this.'

Satisfied with the snake-in-a-shoe picture, Albert discusses technique. He sees himself, above all, as a craftsman. Technique is of the utmost importance to him. Albert does not believe in happy accidents, although he finds photography a highly emotional experience. 'We keep a complete archive of all the shots taken over the past fifteen years. I think it's very important to keep a mental and written record on a daily basis. We keep polaroids for easy reference. It's very important to record just how you achieved certain shots as well as to be able to mark progress in your own development. The idea is, every year, to become a better photographer.' Albert believes in self control. 'I admit I hate it when a young photographer comes round and says "don't you ever have any fun". I suppose my approach to photography does seem a little military. But it gets the results I want.'

In a small atrium at the end of the studio is this Carrara marble statue of an angel by the nineteenth-century Italian sculptor Antonio Angenti.

This is the image Albert singled out from
those he took for the Fabrice assignment.
Albert felt that by having Pam's back
facing the camera there is more mystery
and romance in the picture. The 6 x 6
transparency was taken on *Professional
Ecktachrome* using a Hasselblad and a
single source of artificial light.

Albert's photograph of the snake entwined in
the snakeskin shoe, taken to advertise the work
of shoe designers Susan Bennis and Warren
Edwards. A powerful image, it relies not on
gimmicky propping or lighting but on the
simple visual pun of live and dead snake. The
arrangement of the snake into a 'shoelace' took
hours of coaxing.

DAVID A. BAILEY IN LONDON

David A. Bailey is a young London photographer. He takes many style-oriented photographs, but unlike most photographers in this field he sees his work as political and narrative rather than merely a way of conveying new styles and images. David believes that black people are still too often presented as stereotypes and that his job is to help alter this perspective.

'Blacks are nearly always shown as athletes, musicians or dancers', says David. 'In fashion pictures the black guys are always very muscular.' In other words the images we see of black people in magazines are not only hackneyed, but continually reinforce the stereotype.

'We're used to seeing black people in particular situations, often threatening ones', says David. 'In the early eighties the most common images of black people in the media were those taken during the Brixton or Toxteth riots.' David feels that black people are shown as a foil to white people. Magazine editors choose to show them as dangerous outsiders or as alien figures. 'You rarely see black people doing normal things. In America, for example, where there is a considerable amount of integration, the situation is very different. In Britain black people are still portrayed as wild and exotic. The whole process of photographing and publishing images of blacks is a kind of fantasy, voyeurism if you like.'

'BLACK PEOPLE ARE ALWAYS PRESENTED STEREOTYPICALLY IN THE MEDIA — EVEN IF THOSE IMAGES ARE SUPPOSED TO BE POSITIVE, THEY ARE CATEGORISED INTO CERTAIN TYPES — THE ATHLETE, DANCER OR COMEDIAN.'

Above: Model Rexford and me dramatically lit from underneath by a single lamp on the floor of David A. Bailey's studio.

Below: David in action photographing the four mannequins. His lighting is, appropriately, pure film noire.

David's interest in photography developed at school where cameras were used as working tools during physics lessons. Occasionally the teachers would encourage the children to develop the films themselves. The process fascinated David and he began to explore the possibilities of photography and printing at a youth club in Camden during the evenings. He began teaching other children when he was thirteen (he is twenty-six now), and his teenage work featured in a touring exhibition 'Blacks in Britain'. David went on to study sociology at Sussex University. His thesis on the way photographers are conditioned to see made extensive use of his own photographs.

According to David, 'photographs lie all the time'. 'All photographers manipulate reality. Realism is socially constructed.' I asked David if there could be a recognisable black photography as there is black music, for example. 'Not really. What matters is that black photographers should create images of black people that break away from the stereotypes. They should normalise blacks, look at the possibilities of blurring the edges. A lot of African music, to use an analogy, has been influenced by European and American sounds and a lot of rock music by black rhythms. It's integration that produces some of the most interesting music or images. At the moment things are still at the stage where someone commissioning a black photographer knows what's in their portfolio before they open it. If I showed some landscape work alongside prints of black kids on the streets, nine times out of ten I would be commissioned to photograph the kids.'

'THE PROJECT "BLACKS IN BRITAIN" CHANGED MY PERCEPTIONS OF PHOTOGRAPHY AND MADE ME THINK ABOUT WHY I'M TAKING IMAGES AND WHO I AM TAKING THEM FOR. I LIKE TO QUESTION AND EXPLORE VARIOUS IMAGES AND PRECONCEPTIONS.'

When I went to visit David at his studio he was working on an exploratory photograph using a black model, Rexford, to undermine stereotypes of black and white. Rexford moved through a set dominated by four, blank-faced, white mannequins. The model's hair was slicked back and dyed white. He wore green contact lenses to lighten the colour of his eyes on black and white film. 'This will create a really ambiguous feeling to the picture. Who's black and who's white within all of this.'

Does David ever expect to see his narrative approach to photography ever appearing in magazines like *Vogue*? 'It's a difficult question. I think my work questions the way magazines represent

black and white people. There's fashion as shown in a magazine and then there's actually what's fashionable. I would like to be in a situation where my work would be so fashionable that it would be in the magazines, rather than for photographer and commissioning art editor to look for an acceptable compromise.'

David shooting from low down with a tripod-mounted Canon AT-1. David's photographs on this session were very dramatic, making use of chiaroscuro effects that emphasise both a distinction and blurring of black and white subject matter. The point of the session was to question what and who defines black or white.

FAMILY PORTRAIT. *David believes blacks are portrayed too often as 'athletes or rioters'. In this portrait he makes a point of normalising his subjects and of getting away from the image of exotic aliens. 'We're used to seeing black people in threatening situations.'*

BOY AGAINST RAILINGS. *A powerful graphic*
image using available natural light to
re-create the same high contrast effect that
David achieves in the studio with lights.
The model fuses with the railings and
undertones of a crucified form are
inescapable.

David's chosen image from the session.
Rexford, the model, has been made up so
that there is a mix-up in his racial identity.
He pops out from the group of white
mannequins posed against a brooding black
and white backdrop. The powerful shadows
were created using a single light source, a
lamp positioned on the floor with baffles to
concentrate the effect.

*Rexford's face is contrasted in this image
against the bleached-out profile of a
mannequin's head. Again David makes use
of a single light source, high contrast and a
low camera angle.*

CHAPTER THREE

THE STAMP OF APPROVAL

HRH THE DUKE OF YORK ON A SECRET COMMISSION.

If you are old enough, or if you ever collected stamps, you should remember the set of high value stamps from the mid-1950s depicting British castles. These featured romantic engravings of Windsor, Edinburgh, Carrickfergus and Caernarfon castles, representing England, Scotland, Northern Ireland and Wales, the four countries that together form the United Kingdom. At a time when special commemorative stamps were few and far between, these impressive, standard-issue stamps were among the most collectable.

The Penny Black, the world's first postage stamp, came into use in 1840. A hundred and fifty years on, the Post Office decided to issue a new set of high-value stamps printed in exactly the same way as the Penny Blacks, stamps that would feature new illustrations of Edinburgh, Windsor, Caernarfon and Carrickfergus. With the plan agreed, the next decision was the choice of an illustrator. The Post Office approached, most appropriately, HRH the Duke of York, Prince Andrew, a keen amateur photographer. Windsor is, of course, one of the royal homes.

Because of the Prince's tight schedule much of the preparation work had to be undertaken by the Post Office's Director of Design, Barry Robinson, and myself as photographic adviser to the Prince. The job was particularly demanding as Barry Robinson required extremely detailed shots from which his engraver could work. In other words we had to find the right weather, the exact time of day, keep to a particular view and hope that the Prince would be there. However, we got there and the result of Prince Andrew's work can be judged from the new stamps put into circulation in autumn 1988.

Prince Andrew has not been a photographer for very long, but he has shown tremendous enthusiasm for his hobby. He was instrumental in choosing Albert Watson as the official photographer at his wedding to Sarah Ferguson. He even managed to wish Watson good luck before setting off for the service. Perhaps his most significant role as a photographer, and the one that both today's media and future historians will always be interested in, are his photographs of the various members of the Royal Family.

Prince Andrew first took photography seriously when I invited him to take part in my Personal Points of View exhibition. His work was then accepted for the 1985 Ilford Calendar. I asked the Prince if he felt that he was chosen less because he is a good photographer and more because he is a famous personality. 'I'm not quite sure why Ilford chose me', he replied modestly. 'I think partly because perhaps I may be somebody that people are interested in. I think Ilford also wants to promote the art of photography to other people and show that amateurs can do it.'

The photographs were presented to the selection board at Ilford with only one of the directors knowing who took which picture. The whole idea was to choose photographs strictly on merit. Ten out of twelve said yes to the Prince's portfolio. The other photographs in the Calendar were mostly taken in settings that the Prince knew well: Windsor, Balmoral and Sandringham. Knowing the locations helped the Prince to use them to their best advantage, avoiding the obvious views that tourists automatically take.

Some of Prince Andrew's best photographs are those he has taken of other members of the Royal Family. Those of the Duchess of York and the one of Her Majesty the Queen on her sixtieth birthday are some of the most informal and yet sympathetic views. Prince Andrew remains diffident. Certainly his position enables him to take candid photographs of the Royal Family, pictures that if he were minded to he could sell to the press across the globe. But is he interested, I asked, in developing a career as a photographer or will it remain purely a hobby?

'I don't see myself as a flag waver for photography at all', the Prince says. 'I take personal photographs that people might want to use. I would prefer to continue photography as a hobby rather than as an active professional. I don't want to take any type of work away from anyone else who is more capable of doing it than I am.' So how did the Prince feel about the commission for the new postage stamps? 'I'm very happy to do this particular set of stamps because of my various connections; it's not inappropriate for me to do so.'

Modesty and pressures of time aside, if Prince Andrew were so minded to set up as a full-time photographer there would be no shortage of sitters for his portraits. Yet the Duke of York's favourite subject is very much at home. I asked if there was one particular person he would like to photograph given an unlimited choice. His reply? 'Oh, I think undoubtedly Sarah. I think I have a certain flair and relationship with Sarah that will produce a photograph that nobody else could.'

SELF-PORTRAIT OF PRINCE ANDREW
taken at Buckingham Palace for the exhibition
Personal Points of View, *1985, using*
available light and a Nikon FE2.

SARAH FERGUSON, 1986. *Now the Duchess of York, Sarah is her husband's favourite photographic subject. Her strong natural colouring makes her a perfect choice for a colour portrait. The picture was taken with a large format Hasselblad.*

HER MAJESTY THE QUEEN. *The official
sixtieth birthday photograph of the Queen
taken at Sandringham. This unusually relaxed
portrait shows the Queen as a monarch and
mother, not so difficult when the man behind
the 150mm lens is her son. The photograph
was taken using artificial light and a 6 x 6
format Hasselblad.*

INTERIOR OF ST. GEORGE'S CHAPEL,
WINDSOR *with Dean Mann, taken with a
Nikon FE2 and using available light. This
photograph is memorable for the shaft of light
that shone across the Dean of Windsor's face at
the precise moment that Prince Andrew
released the shutter, proving that luck in a
good photograph can play as great a part
as technical judgement.*

'THE NINTH WIFE' *is a ghostly image of the dancer and actress Finola Hughes. This double exposure photograph was conjured up in the abandoned and pitch black escape tunnel leading from the Curfew Tower at Windsor Castle to the Thames. The underground session took three hours to set up and was recorded on a 4 x 5 Sinar.*

THE 'COPPER HORSE'. *This statue at Windsor Castle portrays Queen Victoria on a charger. This dramatic silhouette was taken using a Nikon FE2 and was one of the photographs selected for the 1985 Ilford Calendar, which made exclusive use*

THE QUEEN WITH ONE OF HER CORGIES.
*An informal, grainy image of the Queen
caught walking one of her corgies across a
deserted and blustery beach. Being part of
the royal family, Prince Andrew has been
able to portray the Queen in casual
moments unavailable to professional
photographers. He used a Nikon FE2.*

PRINCE ANDREW CAPTURES THE CASTLES

Commissioning a Royal Prince is one thing. Trying to fit into his hectic schedule, while keeping the enterprise a secret from the press, was quite another. But the timetable was met and Prince Andrew's photographs now grace the brand-new set of stamps.

How did the project get off the ground? Back in the spring of 1986, Prince Andrew and Sarah Ferguson were invited to view the printing of the special-issue stamp designed to commemorate their forthcoming Royal Wedding. During the visit to the specialist stamp printers, Harrisons & Sons Ltd, I made the casual suggestion that the Prince's own interest in photography might one day be used in helping to produce a set of stamps. That suggestion prompted Keith Fisher, General Manager of the Post Office, to write to the Duke asking if he would like to photograph four British castles for reproduction on a new set of high-value stamps.

With the Duke's enthusiasm and approval from Buckingham Palace, plans were made to photograph the individual castles. Barry and I visited each of the castle sites beforehand to research and prepare for the real thing. I took preliminary photographs of the castles from every possible angle while Barry made meticulous notes about the time of day and camera positions.

If the Duke of York had been a commercial photographer there would have been little difficulty in organising the assignment. But getting a well-known figure like Prince Andrew to click away outside such popular tourist spots as Windsor, Edinburgh and Caernarfon castles was rather like asking the Queen to shop unnoticed in Harrods. Members of the Royal Family attract a crowd wherever they go. Everything had to be done with as little publicity as possible to ensure the success of the project and the personal security of Prince Andrew.

The castle we thought would be the most accessible and easiest to photograph was, in fact, left until last. Scaffolding on the famous Round Tower could not be removed until March 1988.

One of the possible views of Edinburgh Castle that might have been selected. Although dramatic we would have to use a horizontal format for the stamp and so this angle seemed inappropriate.

Prince Andrew at work photographing Carrickfergus Castle early one morning when no one was about (above). This view of Carrickfergus Castle (below) was the one we eventually chose after a careful study of possible alternatives. A Hasselblad 500CM was used.

Above: Prince Andrew, in company with Tom King, Secretary of State for Northern Ireland, examines a set of the original castle stamps at Carrickfergus.

Above: Close-up of an original castle stamp dating from the early 1950s. Prince Andrew's assignment over thirty years later was to provide the Post Office with a fresh set of images for the new high-value castle stamps which went on sale in autumn 1988.

The rest of the shots were taken the previous autumn and went ahead – almost smoothly.

Edinburgh was simple enough. There the only difficulty was finding the perfect time of day for photography and a time when few tourists were about. We chose a Sunday morning, although as we were all being filmed for television, we would naturally attract some attention whether the Duke of York was there or not.

The logistics now seemed clear. But there was still the weather to contend with. In fact, we could hardly have chosen a worse day for Edinburgh. It was the night of the storms, the worst to hit Britain since 1708. Barry Robinson of the Post Office and I had done our homework meticulously. The photograph of Edinburgh Castle had to be taken in the early afternoon from Princes' Gardens. Prince Andrew would be staying at Balmoral and would drive himself down. But, when the morning came, I was awoken by the sound and force of one of the fiercest gales in British history screaming through my open hotel window. It was four o'clock in the morning.

> 'IT WAS ABSOLUTELY TEEMING WITH RAIN. THE CAR LEAKED, THE ANTI-LOCK BRAKES FAILED AND IT WAS BLOWING A HOWLING GALE. THERE WAS NO POINT IN TAKING THE PHOTOGRAPH. TWO OR THREE WEEKS LATER WE WERE BACK. IN FACT IT RAINED WHILE WE WERE THERE, BUT IT WAS STILL QUITE GOOD.'

At a quarter to six the bedside phone rang. It was Prince Andrew. He had left Balmoral an hour earlier, but with so many trees down and such foul weather he had made little headway. There was nothing for it but to cancel and make plans for the next possible date.

One of the principal criteria in photographing such a large building is to be able to close in enough to capture the essence of the building as well as sufficient detail for the engraving that would take place in the Post Office design studio later on. It was also very important to produce an image that would be instantly recognisable to the majority of people buying the stamps.

> 'EVERYBODY HAS THEIR PERSONAL VIEW OF AN INDIVIDUAL PIECE OF ART. I LIKE CERTAIN THINGS OTHER PEOPLE DON'T LIKE.'

The problem is compounded in the 1980s by the interminable array of incidental objects obscuring historic buildings. The further back the camera, the more telegraph poles, street lamps and so on get in the way. Although, as we were to see later, Chris Matthews the engraver was able to remove relatively unobtrusive details from the image when he set about his minute engraving, larger objects presented a real difficulty – if they were removed it would be almost impossible to add in the details they hid.

Edinburgh Castle, for example, although massive, broods on a great volcanic rock over four hundred feet high. Getting the camera back far enough to capture the scene can easily mean that the details and texture of its thousand-year-old walls are lost. We had no intention of using a wide angle lens on any of the four photographs, as this would have distorted the image.

Carrickfergus presented the most demanding challenge. We did hope to have Prince Andrew fly out privately, take the pictures on a quiet afternoon and get home without causing too much fuss. Then his trip was combined with an official visit to open the Carrickfergus Marina. With Prince Andrew's tight schedule in mind, it was decided that he should photograph Caernarfon Castle in the morning and then fly across to Carrickfergus, where he would shoot the Ulster castle after opening the marina.

When the day arrived to photograph Caernarfon, Barry and I met Prince Andrew, as arranged, in the castle car park at seven in the morning. Save for a solitary man walking his dog, who took no notice of us, there was not a soul about. As the Prince set up his medium format Hasselblad, Barry suggested a headline for the tabloid press: 'While Caernarfon Sleeps the Prince Clicks'. In fact the press knew absolutely nothing about the trip.

The picture we took was not the one originally intended. During our reconnaissance, a large boat dominated a particularly fine view of the castle from the footbridge across the River Seiont. But on the day the Prince arrived, our luck was in and the boat was out. We all wanted a photograph that would best show the magnificent reflections of the castle in the waters that surround it. As at Edinburgh we took no chances with

Below: Here at Caernarfon Castle I am discussing the light conditions and angle of the photograph with Prince Andrew. The images were taken on square format film and the aim, despite the weather, was to get the sharpest possible negative.

We tried several views of Caernarfon Castle. Some were crowded with incidental clutter while others failed to capture the magical possibilities offered by reflections from the surrounding waters. This (above right) is one of the angles we rejected; the view below fitted all the criteria and was recorded by Prince Andrew in the final photograph.

the vagaries of light and weather. Prince Andrew used all the filters available to ensure the perfect picture. It would be very unlikely that he would find time to return and meanwhile the engraver needed a photograph that revealed as much clear detail as possible.

> 'I HAVE A BAD HABIT OF TAKING
> TWO PHOTOGRAPHS ALL THE TIME,
> MOSTLY AS INSURANCE.'

We packed up and flew on to Carrickfergus, the maritime fortress built at the end of the twelfth century by John de Courcy, the Norman conqueror of Ulster. Captured by King John in 1210 it remained an English garrison until 1928. While Prince Andrew descended into the crowds I waited and checked his equipment. At Carrickfergus it was impossible to keep the crowds away and for that reason we had to work very quickly.

With Carrickfergus safely on film we now had to wait over the winter for the scaffolding to come down at Windsor. Prince Andrew contrasted the ease with which he was able to take photographs at Windsor compared to the situation at Carrickfergus.

> 'BEING HEAVILY INVOLVED WITH
> THE NAVY MEANS I CAN'T ACTUALLY
> SPEND TIME DOING THE LEG WORK,
> APART FROM WINDSOR WHICH IS OF
> COURSE HOME TERRITORY.'

'Certainly nobody took any notice of us at Windsor because there was a gentleman who appeared with a camera and stood in front of us for fifteen minutes and never took a photograph. The next thing that happened is that he walked behind us and took a photograph over our shoulders, the same picture that we'd just taken. And I don't think he realised who we were. I think he just wanted to have our spot.

'At Carrickfergus the whole situation was entirely different. There were about forty officers of the RUC (Royal Ulster

Constabulary) hiding behind various rocks and pillars and boats for the duration of the shot.'

Finally it was time to transform Prince Andrew's photographs into engravings. The craft involved in transferring a photographic image into an intaglio print (a high-quality and traditional method of printing rarely used today except for Bank of England notes) is not only painstaking, but allows no room for error. It is a complex and time-consuming process and one that the Prince was keen to grasp.

Prince Andrew at work (above) photographing Windsor Castle. The test shot (below) was taken in autumn 1987 when scaffolding still surrounded the *Round Tower. This was finally removed in March 1988, when the Prince was able to set up his Hasselblad for the definitive image seen on page 68.*

MAKING THE STAMPS

Intaglio printing is rarely used now by the Post Office on a regular basis, but it is a process that European printers used for five hundred years. An artist like Albrecht Durer, the fifteenth-century German, would have been quite at home in the Harrisons' workshop.

Prince Andrew visited Harrisons, the printers, to watch the process that would turn prints taken from his original 6cm by 6cm negatives into the miniature images necessary for the stamps. A skilled engraver, in this case Chris Matthews, has the eye-straining job of reproducing Prince Andrew's prints through a multiplicity of minute lines and cross-hatches on to a steel plate. Matthews has to do this in reverse, looking through an eye glass. He will work for up to twelve hours at a stretch. This miniature work requires immense concentration and he cannot afford to make a single mistake. If he does he will have to start from scratch working on a fresh plate.

When the plate is engraved it is smeared with a rather sticky ink which fills the sunken lines created by the steel engraver. The surface is wiped clean before it is ready for printing. To add a second and further colours the plate has to be washed and loaded again with fresh ink.

But if the engraver is really drawing each of the historic castles from scratch each time, then, as Prince Andrew asked, why bother with the photographs? Chris Matthews explained that while it is possible to work from a drawing or painting, a photograph is much better as it shows more detail. Barry Robinson wanted the images on the new stamps to appear as realistic as possible and so high-contrast photographs were essential. Chris Matthews discussed the print of Edinburgh Castle with the Prince.

'Whereas an artist will have, say, just one little brush stroke for a certain area, here I can actually see the individual rocks.' Even with an eye piece to magnify the plate six times to assist him, it takes Matthews nearly three weeks to

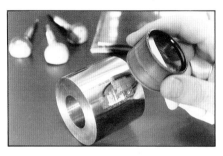

finish the image of Edinburgh Castle. 'You have to keep referring to the photograph', Matthews told the Prince; 'my job is to convert a tonal picture into lines so that when it prints it has the same effect as the original'. A variety of line widths and depths produces a range of effects from sharply defined detail to areas of tone. Once the first print is made there is still room for minor adjustment; a few more lines and hatches. But if the result were really unsatisfactory, then Matthews would have to start all over again. With a strict timetable to be met, he simply cannot afford to slip up.

What the engraver chooses to add in or leave out of the Prince's prints is never left to whim. The reasons are always practical. Some of the lamp posts which show in Prince Andrew's print of Carrickfergus are omitted from the engraving. Matthews explains that they would have clashed with the Queen's portrait.

The Prince's next question was one that any photographer pleased with their handiwork would want to ask. 'What advantage is there from using a photograph and then making it into an engraving as opposed to just printing a photograph as a stamp?' Matthews replied that, although the stamps could have been produced with litho or photo-

The photographic image is carefully copied on to the stamp plate using a myriad of tiny engraved lines, visible under the magnifying glass but quite unnoticeable on the finished stamp.

gravure processes, intaglio was the most difficult process for forgers to copy.

If it seems odd that one of the oldest forms of printing illustrations should also be the best for preventing forgery, what has to be remembered is the role of the individual craftsman. To produce a convincing replica of the stamp photographed by Prince Andrew, designed by Barry Robinson and engraved by Chris Matthews, the forger has got to slavishly adhere to Matthew's painstaking labour. A few hiccups here and there and the forgery would be easy to spot. The intaglio process is also offputting to would-be forgers because it is so time-consuming.

Because the stamps are printed directly from the original engraving, each stamp could be said to come straight from the craftsman's work, unlike other printing processes. This does mean that very slight differences can occur between individual stamps; although this is of course something the printers try to avoid, it is often of interest to stamp collectors.

All that remained to be done was to print the final approved engraving on Post Office-issue numbered and gummed paper. The results were available for the public to judge from October 18th 1988.

Prince Andrew's vision of Windsor Castle translated into one of the new series of high-value Post Office stamps. As in all four stamps, the engraver, working from the photographic print, has chosen to omit certain extraneous details such as telephone wires and street lamps.

The Windsor Castle stamp.

Edinburgh Castle: the final image. Our first attempt met with dismal failure when we set a date that coincided nicely with the great storm of autumn 1987, so that Prince Andrew was unable to drive from Balmoral to the Scottish capital. The weather improved for our second photo session when Prince Andrew took this classic picture from Princes' Street Gardens.

The Edinburgh Castle stamp.

Caernarfon Castle: the final image. We had to take this photograph early in the morning to give Prince Andrew enough time and privacy to work. A famous photographer often attracts a lot of attention, but a royal photographer could encourage the whole town to come down and take a look.

The Caernarfon Castle stamp.

As with Caernarfon Castle, Carrickfergus is surrounded by water, but it is also adjacent to a new marina. This had to be excluded from view as the most important consideration was to create a timeless image of the castle. Because of the high-value nature of the stamps and the fact that they would possibly not be replaced for another twenty years, an image had to be found that generated a feeling of timeless authenticity.

The Carrickfergus Castle stamp.

CHAPTER FOUR

NATURAL HISTORY SAFARI

HEATHER ANGEL, BRILLIANT NATURAL HISTORY PHOTOGRAPHER,
REVEALS SOME TRICKS OF THE TRADE.

Photographing wildlife is one of the most difficult areas of photography. Having said this, anyone with a bit of patience, a single lens reflex camera and a zoom lens should enjoy themselves while being able to capture some memorable shots. But truly inspired wildlife photography requires not only infinite patience and plenty of time, but also a thorough knowledge of animals, plants, their habitat and behaviour.

I went to talk to Heather Angel, one of the world's top nature photographers, at work in her Surrey studio and on location in the New Forest. Heather made it clear that you do not need exotic locations to find unusual creatures. Even some of Britain's commoner animals are so elusive that to be able to capture them on camera is a major achievement. A good photograph of a badger is something any professional wildlife photographer would be proud of.

Heather stressed that disturbing animals is not only wrong, but will prevent an amateur from ever capturing an animal behaving normally on film. Patience, camouflage, silence and an ability to remain still for long spells are just as important as the equipment you own. Heather suggests that those taking up nature photography for the first time should begin practising their technique in parks and gardens. Squirrels and many birds allow you to approach quite closely, while a bird bath and a buddleia in your garden will attract a surprising variety of birds and butterflies even in city centres.

If photographing any animal indoors or in the studio, Heather stresses that its welfare must always come first. Never persist, she says, in taking a picture if the subject shows signs of distress. As you can see there are a lot of ifs and buts, dos and don'ts in nature photography. I approached Heather Angel's studio in suitably hushed tones.

Heather Angel's interest in wildlife was partly stimulated by visits to her grandparents' Suffolk farm. She had a peripatetic childhood, as her father was an RAF officer and the family was constantly on the move. Heather attended no less than fourteen schools (three in New Zealand alone), yet her education hardly suffered. She took a degree in Zoology at Bristol University in 1962 and followed this with an MSc three years later.

Heather is self-taught as a photographer. She insists that as a child she never handled a camera. It was during her university research that she began to use photography, but only for factual records. She went on an underwater expedition to Norway with her husband Martin Angel, an oceanographer, when she was twenty-one and thought it best to take a camera. Since then she has won all sorts of awards and medals for her nature photography and was President of The Royal Photographic Society from 1984 to 1986 (only the second woman in one hundred and thirty years).

Heather has published an astonishing thirty-eight books on nature and photography since 1972, the combined sales of which top three quarters of a million. She travels extensively, appears on radio and television, is sought after as a lecturer, has put on or been featured in six major exhibitions, runs a photographic library comprising well over a quarter of a million transparencies and manages, somehow, to be a perfectly normal – or perhaps extraordinary – wife and mother to her eleven-year-old son Giles. Her most recent books include *Heather Angel's Countryside* (1983), *A Camera in the Garden* (1984), *A View from a Window* and *Nature in Focus* (1988). She has contributed a regular column on nature photography to *Camera Weekly* since 1967.

Being successful in her own field takes Heather to many exotic locations. Recently she has worked in China, Kenya and Mexico. Her trips have to be self-financing. She pumps her earnings from selling photographs, books and magazine articles back into travel so that she can take more photographs.

Although Heather organises many of her own trips and sorts out her own finance, she also takes on commissioned work. In recent years she has enjoyed some particularly satisfying commissions. The Italian magazine *Gardenis* took her to Ruwenzori (Mountains of the Moon) in Uganda to photograph the bizarre plants peculiar to this exotic location, and she became a royal photographer for a day when *Natural World* magazine asked her to photograph the Prince of Wales in the flower meadow at Highgrove on the occasion of the launch of the British Wildlife Appeal.

Some of Heather's finest photographs have been reproduced many times. The wonderfully graphic image of the bright green and yellow Costa Rican flying frog was taken twelve years ago. It is one of Heather's favourite (and best-selling) shots. She showed me one of her most exciting photographs, taken on location in Sri Lanka when Heather's stationary jeep was being charged by a bull elephant. As is usual with a professional photographer, Heather was so intent on getting a good picture that she was hardly aware of the danger. Fortunately for Heather, elephant and jeep, the angry animal lost interest half-way through its charge and slunk off into the jungle.

FLYING FROG (AGALYCHNIS SPURRELLI).
This much-travelled frog was brought from
Costa Rica by the BBC Natural History Unit,
and returned after a flight sequence had been
filmed. Heather persuaded the frog to leap on
to a sheet of glass to show the large suction
pads on its feet. She used a flash for this
studio shot taken with a Hasselblad.

BABY GREY WHALE *(ESCHRICHTIUS*

FLOWERING MARSH MARIGOLDS
*(CALTHA PALUSTRIS) enlivened a wet
meadow near Maenturog in Wales. This
was a completely unplanned shot taken while
Heather was driving around looking for local
subjects for an exhibition of her work to be
shown at Aberystwyth Arts Centre in 1986.
She used a wide-angle 50mm lens on a
Hasselblad and shot against the light.*

SILVER BIRCH *(BETULA PENDULA)*
CATKINS. *This graphic studio shot depicts
wind pollination. Heather used two flashes*

EARTH STAR (GEASTRUM TRIPLEX). This
studio photograph of an earth star dispersing a
spore cloud is one of Heather's best-selling
plant pictures because it depicts action.
Her husband was simulating rain by
dropping water from a pipette out of shot!
She used a Hasselblad with extension tubes
and three flashes (two behind and one as a
fill-in in front).

HEATHER ANGEL ON LOCATION

I went to visit Heather Angel at her home in Surrey, where she planned to photograph a strange collection of exotic insects and fish in her studio. In contrast, her next assignment took place in the wilds of the New Forest. I accompanied her to see how it was done.

Heather Angel's studio is a rustic potting shed hidden in a hollow in her land-scaped Surrey garden. On my visit Heather was busy setting up a shot of tropical fish. This might sound very easy, but how do you photograph an aquarium without reflections?

Heather places her camera on a tripod behind a matt black board. A sheet of black Formica is placed inside the back of the tank to cut out the studio background. Heather lights the aquarium from the top to simulate sunlight and to avoid unnatural shadows being cast by rocks and weeds.

All we have to do now is wait for the fish to swim past the lens in an interesting group. If they refuse to budge, then Heather recommends a pinch of food and not a surreptitious prod. It is also important to find plants that look authentic. The fish Heather was photographing – including Siamese Fighting Fish and, appropriately, Angel Fish – were tropical and for this photo-graph she was keen to ensure a realistic effect.

Heather then photographed a horned frog and a tarantula before we had to

'I LOOK VERY CAREFULLY AT THE BACKGROUND IN RELATION TO THE SUBJECT, HOW IT'S LIT, AND MAY GET INTO A TORTUOUS CAMERA POSITION IN ORDER TO GET A BETTER SHOT.'

break off to look at proofs of her latest book. This is one of the most important processes for any photographer. A photographer might take consistently excellent pictures, yet the images the public see are always at least one stage removed from the initial transparencies. A book or magazine publisher can either reproduce a photographer's work accur-ately or demean it. Often a photo-

grapher's work is judged on how the reproduction on the printed page looks. So Heather examines the colour proofs with a studied eye.

Four-colour printing means exactly that. All colour photographs are recreated on a page by mixing magenta, yellow, cyan and black. A slight variation in any of these will greatly affect the warmth or depth of a particular shot. This is especially important for Heather as she looks at images that were difficult to capture in the first place, such as an eagle photographed in a snowstorm. The colour processing has to be spot-on to capture the subtlety of Heather's original transparency.

Left: Heather Angel with the Thames Television crew and Martin Noble, a Head Forester with the Forestry Commission, on location in the New Forest early in June. We were filming a sequence demonstrating the use of a polarising filter to remove skylight reflections from the water surface. The subject was water crowfoot flowers in a shallow pond. Heather had come well prepared with her waders.

Right: Heather fixes a Hasselblad — complete with a 250mm lens — to her versatile Benbo tripod ready to photograph deer at Bolderwood. Notice the variety of cameras, lenses and film at the ready in the open rucksack. Preferring fixed focal length lenses to zooms, she loses count of the number of times she changes lenses in a day.

We spent a morning in the New Forest together. Heather says that she finds as much to record here as she does on the Galapagos Islands. She simply forgets herself, and eats and sleeps when she can. What matters is to wait for the situation where she can be sure of a memorable photograph. The day we chose was not ideal for photography. The fallow deer turned out in force (there are about eighteen hundred to choose from in the New Forest) but it was a dark morning and Heather needed to work with a very fast film (800 ISO) while opening up the lens to as much as f2.8. A fast film will mean rather grainy pictures and Heather is not at all keen on these for wildlife photography. In any case, when she is photographing for a book she needs to use films, whatever the lighting conditions, that are compatible in effect. If you came across a grainy picture in a book of otherwise crystal-clear images it would stand out like a sore thumb.

Light levels are always unpredictable in Britain, especially when, as Heather does, a photographer will insist on going on location at the crack of dawn. As Heather says, she has the satisfaction of getting through a hard day's work when most people are sitting down to breakfast. This, as we discovered, is the time when you are most likely to find mammals moving freely. Later in the day they begin to hide or sleep, only coming out in the evening when again the light is low and photography more difficult.

Heather is never frugal with film and even when taking a static subject in constant light she will shoot at least half a dozen frames, since an original transparency is always much better quality than any duplicate. If the light level is fluctuating, however, and she is taking a landscape, she will vary the exposure slightly to be sure of getting at least one winner.

On this trip Heather races through five rolls in as many minutes. She is constantly amazed by how mean many amateurs are with film – the cheapest part of the photographic process. Many spend a small fortune on equipment and yet go out with just a few rolls of film. This often proves to be galling for the photographer who often discovers the best angles later in the day, particularly once a subject has become familiar.

Heather does stress, however, that to get the close-ups we all admire you will need a variety of lenses, none of which come cheap. A 400mm telephoto lens is essential for close-ups of smaller animals in the wild. As Heather explained, most animals have a much keener sense of smell than humans and unless you know how to get downwind of a deer, fox or rabbit, it will scamper into the undergrowth well before a standard 50mm lens could bring the animal any closer than one seen through the wrong end of a telescope.

With the deer captured on film we went off to photograph adders, not an animal anyone should get too close to – they are unlikely to kill, but their bite is painful and debilitating – before calling it a day. Our trip showed that the working day of a wildlife photographer can only be organised up to a point. On a fashion session, Albert Watson can ask a model to pose the way he wants, although of course out of the studio he too is dependent on the weather. But Heather Angel is very much in the hands, or hoofs or paws, of the animals she stalks.

However, Heather's remarkable output shows what can be done with masses of enthusiasm, boundless patience and a detailed knowledge of botany and zoology. Heather Angel's working day certainly exhausted me.

Above: Heather merges into the forest surroundings by donning this portable camouflage hide.

Above: To show the full height of this old pollarded beech tree, a 50mm lens had to be used on a Hasselblad.

Above: Heather waits patiently for fallow deer (DAMA DAMA) to move in closer towards her. If they don't oblige, she will swap over to a longer lens.

Above: Heather and me in a permanent Forestry Commission hide at dawn, waiting for the animals to appear.

Right: Using waders, Heather can safely work in mid-water taking close-ups of water crowfoot flowers using a 105mm macro lens on her Nikon.

Tropical freshwater fish, taken in an aquarium planted with tropical water weeds in Heather Angel's studio. A single overhead flash was used to simulate natural sunlight shining through water and a matt black mask fitted to the front of the camera lens prevented any reflections appearing in the front glass.

*An immature South American horned frog
(CERATOPHRYS) belies the huge size it will
eventually reach, with a prominent horn
above each eye. Studio Multiblitz flash
with built-in modelling lights suspended
from an overhead gantry were used to
check where the shadow would fall before
making the exposure.*

Heather used strong side lighting from a studio flash to accentuate the hairiness of this tarantula spider from Chile. Most of the crew were highly relieved it did not escape from the glass-fronted vivarium during the filming hession! It is photographed on a piece of bark which virtually filled the background.

These fallow deer (DAMA DAMA) were
photographed at Bolderwood from a public
raised deer platform (a screen with viewing
slits) using a 300mm lens and Kodachrome
Professional 200. Being wild, the deer are
quite free to move off into the
undergrowth, but they tend to gravitate
back to these fields where they are fed
daily. The males or bucks can be
distinguished by their antlers, and all the
deer are sporting their summer coats.

*Round-leaved sundew (DROSERA
ROTUNDIFOLIA) is one of several
insectivorous plants which grow in the New
Forest bogs. In order to see the detail of the
sticky leaf hairs used for trapping insects, a
macro lens and a firm camera support are
essential, but it usually means ending up
with wet knees to get a decent picture.*

An adder (*VIPERA BERUS*) rests on a boggy
heathland in part of the New Forest. As
the weather was overcast, the snake was
not particularly active, so Heather could
get away with using a fairly slow shutter
speed with a 105mm macro lens on
her Nikon.

Chapter Five

State of the Art

Terence Donovan on the most fashionable images;
Linda McCartney with a more personal approach to the avant-garde.

Both Terence Donovan and Linda McCartney, in their own way, represent the most up-to-date in photography: Donovan in his innovative presentation of the height of fashion; Linda in her exploration of the newest techniques and her innovative, avant-garde images. Both, too, are marketing something, even if rather different – the most current, expensive fashion compared to the English landscape and its heritage. However, as you will read, these concerns are only a part of their wide-ranging photographic interests.

In the 1960s Terence Donovan took fashion photography out of the smart Regency drawing rooms and London park settings so typical of the 1950s and into the street. To see a smartly tailored gentleman's suit photographed against a gasworks or an East End shopping street was something revolutionary twenty-five years ago.

Terence Donovan is the archetypal East End boy made good, an intuitive and highly skilled photographer who has reached the top by approaching each assignment afresh and never resting on his laurels. Although Terence is now heavily involved in television and cinema adverts, pop videos and documentaries, fashion photography is still his métier.

I followed Terence on an assignment for *Vogue*, from the initial meeting with the editorial staff at the magazine's London offices in Hanover Square, through to the actual session in a photographic studio in Holborn and on to the final choice of stills. In between I talked to Terence about his career and also attended a lecture he gave to the Tottenham Camera Club. This showed the easy rapport that Donovan has with people around him, his willingness to pass on tips – many of which go against the grain, challenging the fixation that many manufacturers and amateur photographers have with sophisticated equipment and gadgetry – and his sense of humour.

Linda McCartney also sprang out of the Pop world of the mid-sixties. And, like Donovan, Linda is a very intuitive photographer little interested in gadgetry. However, unlike Donovan, her subjects are landscapes, favourite places, abstracts, friends and local people rather than glamorous, long-legged models. I went to Rye, the picturesque Sussex town, to look at Linda's latest exhibition and to talk to her about her very different approach to photography.

Terence Donovan is famous for his work for fashion magazines such as *Vogue* and *Cosmopolitan*. He has also made over three thousand commercials, a large number of distinguished pop videos (his latest is for Robert Palmer) and television documentaries. One of the most memorable took Clive James on an anthropological exploration of the summer Paris fashion shows. He also took the official photographs (along with myself and Albert Watson) of Prince Andrew and Sarah Ferguson's engagement in 1986.

Donovan was born in Mile End in 1937, the son of a lorry driver and a Woolworth's manageress. At the age of eleven he took a course in blockmaking at the London College of Engraving and Lithography, which helped him get a job four years later in the photographic department of a Fleet Street blockmaker. By then fascinated by photography and with his own dark-room set up at home, Terence says that he was sacked from a job each year before being called up for National Service. He served as an army photographer before setting up on his own.·

An intuitive photographer, Terence does not consider his skill an art form, although he says that 'philosophers could discuss the question for years'. Nor does he think that he has yet made it as a photographer: 'As soon you think that', he says, 'you're on the downward slope'. His prowess at judo and his fascination with Eastern religion and thought has helped him to live from day to day free from professional preconceptions. This freshness showed from the outset in his revolutionary fashion stills in the early sixties.

Editorial features for fashion magazines are not the best-paid work photographers can get, yet magazines like *Vogue* are a good showcase for the talent of a photographer like Terence Donovan. A magazine photo session has to be tightly scheduled, economic and perfect first time round. I joined Donovan on a fashion assignment to see just what was involved.

SEATED MODEL *in low-cut black and gold evening dress, photographed for* Vogue. *Photographs such as this perform a multi-functional role: they advertise not only the clothing but current moods in cosmetics, hairstyling and the general 'look' of the moment.*

GIRL LEANING ON RAIL. *A strategically
placed single light source is combined with an
enigmatic setting to create a sense of timeless
elegance. The choice of black and white rather
than colour for a modern fashion feature is
unusual, but stunningly effective, evoking
early Hollywood glamour portraits. The light
bounces off the wall and rail to outline the
contours of the jacket.*

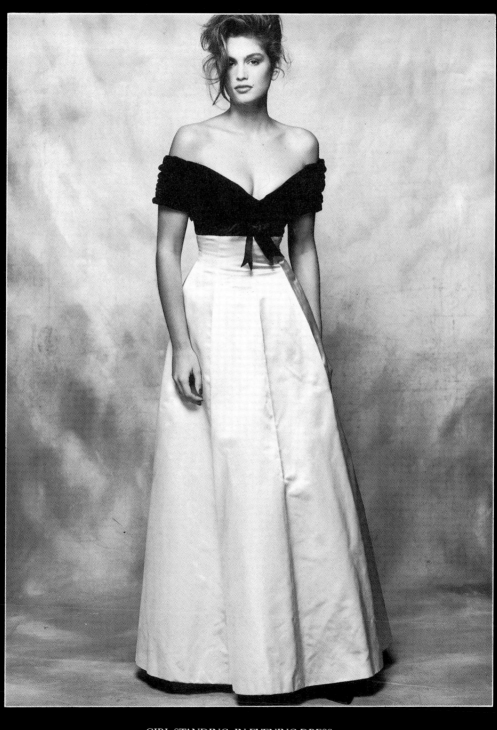

GIRL STANDING, IN EVENING DRESS.
*The subtle sponging of the backdrop forms
a painterly foil to the glowing sheens and
textures of the clothing. Lighting is used to
accentuate the ankle-length princess-cut dress
by creating a pool of shadow at the bottom of
its drop, echoing the border provided by the
swathed black velvet collar.*

STUDY IN GOLD. *A stunning full-length picture, carefully posed and arranged by Donovan down to the last detail, but nonetheless full of freshness and vitality. To achieve this kind of result again and again demands a high degree of visual imagination and sensitivity, to be able to present a never-ending procession of different fashions with variety and enthusiasm.*

MODEL IN PINK DRESS *from a series of
photographs on evening gowns for* Vogue.
*This 'freezing' of the model in mid-movement
is typical of Donovan's style, creating a
dramatic tension between highly-posed
artificiality and a sense of life and action.
The result is a combination of excitement
and glamour.*

TERENCE DONOVAN ON IMAGES IN VOGUE

Interviewing Terence Donovan in front of the television cameras, discussing the role of the fashion photographer for the Thames Television series. (Left.)

Terence Donovan and the television crew set up for the Cara Young/Vogue fashion shoot in the unglamorous basement setting of the Holborn studios. (Above right.)

Underneath the powerful glare of a single high-powered synchronised flash light, Cara adopts her pose while Terence and his assistant Steve prepare to shoot. (Below right.)

Fashion photographs for magazines such as Vogue *need long-term planning. I joined a meeting at Vogue's office in London at the beginning of June involving Terence Donovan and the magazine staff to discuss photography for the December issue. This shows how the fashion trade is always a season ahead. When most people are looking for summer outfits, the fashion business has completed its winter range.*

Elizabeth Tilberis, Editor of Vogue, *wants pictures of eight new dresses by the Emmanuels, who have designed dresses for the Princess of Wales among many other celebrities. Liz, together with her Fashion Editor Anna Harvey and Art Director John Hind, discuss the clothes they want to feature and then begin looking through model portfolios with Donovan and Jo Matthews, the model booker. They choose Cara Young, a beautiful dark-skinned twenty-one year old American. Cara will have to be flown specially from New York to London for the Donovan shoot. Fashion photo-*graphy is quite clearly an expensive business.

'I ALWAYS PREFER TAKING PICTURES IN BLACK AND WHITE AS I THINK THEY'RE MORE DRAMATIC. BUT I USUALLY AM ASKED TO DO COLOUR.'

Terence will look at the clothes, but he says that he never tries to fix a particular photographic approach to an individual designer. 'Fashion photography is about showing clothes for women to wear. It's not to demonstrate great art. It's really about packaging, about information and making the clothes look good. Maybe in some circles people might find that trite, but I don't think it's trite to want to make people look beautiful and feel good.' In fact Terence is very much against the kind of fashion photography, increasingly popular, that shows more of the model than the clothes. 'A good-looking girl is essential, but you're only pretending to do the job if all you can see is a bit of the collar and the rest of the picture is really just a good look at a pretty girl.'

A studio is booked in Holborn for the end of July. Donovan will waste no time. There is a lot to be done and no question of anything going wrong – the magazine needs the pictures and Cara will be flying on to Paris for her next assignment the same evening. The studio is prepared rapidly by two assistants. Terence claims that he has never had a bad assistant, but you get the feeling that anyone not quite up to scratch would be out on their ear in a moment. 'I like assistants who I can train my way. I don't like it if they have preconceived ideas. The worst thing for me on a shoot is when I want something done and someone does something different and says "But, I thought ...". Dangerous words, "'I thought ...'"

'ONCE YOU THINK YOU'VE MADE IT, I THINK YOU'RE ON THE SLOPES. IT'S THE FEELING THAT TOMORROW YOU WILL DO IT BETTER THAT KEEPS YOU GOING.'

The drab studio floor, meanwhile, has become whiter than white. A single,

powerful studio flash is set up and Donovan appears behind the camera – a hi-tech 6 × 8 Fuji GX680 – as Cara emerges, pinned into a glamorous, low-cut black Emmanuel ball gown.

'I'VE NOT FOUND ANYTHING MORE FASCINATING THAN PHOTOGRAPHY. IT'S TOTALLY INTRIGUING – I DON'T THINK I SHALL EVER RETIRE IN THE ORDINARY SENSE OF THE WORD.'

Terence does not like to see the models until they are fully made-up and ready for photographing. He, as usual, is immaculately turned out in a smart grey flannel suit, silk tie and polished black brogues. Despite the background noise of drilling, hammering and motorcycle messengers appearing and disappearing, Donovan works rapidly. The finished photographs will look very glamorous. Yet the process – rapid fire photography

in a great grey hulk of a warehouse studio with hairdressers and make-up artist dressed in jeans and t-shirts – is remarkably prosaic and there are no gimmicks attached.

Terence is able to get the best out of his models partly through his easy rapport with them. 'It's quite lonely for a model out there on a white background under lights after having just flown over three thousand miles for a shoot. It's just common courtesy to be nice to the people you're working with. You can't just treat a model like a donkey in a Christian Dior frock, can you? There has to be a dialogue. I've seen amateurs queuing up to photograph a professional model with their hands shaking. Once you get into a situation like that the model gets uneasy and the whole session is a disaster.' All of which could explain why many top fashion photographers like to work regularly with a few select favourite models.

Cara Young herself seems calm enough. She agrees that a fashion model's life can be a bit lonely at times. There is often too much travelling to very exotic locations. Cara reckons that she

will work for a few more years as a fashion model before taking it easier by posing for catalogues. Her ultimate plans are to get married and have kids. 'It would be nice to lead a normal life after a few more years of this.'

'IT'S A VERY LONELY JOB, PHOTOGRAPHY. YOU MIGHT HAVE A HAIRDRESSER AND MAKE-UP ARTIST AND ASSISTANT, BUT AT THE END OF THE DAY IF YOU HIT A TRICKY PATCH AND CAN'T SOLVE THE PROBLEM YOU ARE ON YOUR OWN.'

In action, Terence Donovan makes photography seem simple. So it was interesting to follow him in the evening to a lecture at the local Tottenham Camera Club to hear what advice he can offer to amateurs. The occasion of Terence's lecture was the fiftieth anniversary of the club. Not surprisingly members turned up in force and packed the community hall. Introduced by Pam Brown, the club's first lady chairman, Donovan perched on the edge of a table

and launched into a fascinating, often hilarious and side-tracking monologue on the art of photography.

'INSTEAD OF ACQUIRING MORE AND MORE PLANT, SELL IT ALL AND JUST GET ONE CAMERA AND ONE LENS. REMEMBER THAT ALL PHOTOGRAPHY IS JUST YOUR REACTION TO SOMETHING.'

'One of the first things you should do', says Donovan, 'is to get rid of all the fancy equipment, the zoom lenses and so on. You need the imagination to free yourself from the gear.' He recommends instead a good basic 35mm SLR camera with a 50mm and possibly 35mm lens and a lot of film. 'To get good you have to take a lot of pictures. It's like judo. You have to practice the same throw fifteen thousand times. It has to become a reflex.'

At the Tottenham Camera Club Terence passes on a number of the 'tricks' of his trade, pointing out, with the aid of photographs such as the one he is showing here to the audience, how a single light source used imaginatively is all that is needed to realise sophisticated fashion portraits. Terence eschews gadgetry in favour of simplicity every time.

Terence Donovan lecturing at the Tottenham Camera Club. His humorous delivery almost belies the years of thought and skill that goes into each of his photographs. But it has earned him a loyal following in his East London homeground, and encourages ambitious amateur photographers to follow in his footsteps. (Left.)

Donovan in action photographing Cara Young. As usual the studio is absolutely bare, and a single studio flash is used for lighting. (Below.)

LINDA MCCARTNEY ON ART AND IMAGES

Like Terence Donovan, Linda McCartney was a product of the Swinging Sixties. Although she set out photographing pop groups, musicians and singers, her natural, intuitive approach led her back to some of her first loves – the countryside, people, surrealism – and on to hand-tints and abstract images.

Linda Eastman, as she then was (and not related to the Kodak Eastmans), was born in New York, majored in art history in Vermont and Arizona and became a photographer purely by accident. While living in Tucson a journalist friend on a local paper encouraged her to enrol at an evening course at the local arts centre. The course, taught by Hazel Archer, opened Linda's eyes to the art of photography. She borrowed a camera, shot off a roll of black and white film (her subjects were horses, dogs and mountains) and was told the results were good. She bought her own camera and kept pressing the shutter.

'I'M A SPONTANEOUS PHOTOGRAPHER. WHATEVER I COME ACROSS, I'LL TAKE A PICTURE OF IT IF IT APPEALS TO ME.'

But it took Linda a while to get into her stride. Moving to New York she took a job as a receptionist with *Town and Country* magazine. One day she pocketed an invitation to a press party to meet the Rolling Stones. She was the only photographer allowed on the boat that sailed up the Hudson River. Not surprisingly journalists were keen for her pictures and that was the way her professional career took off. As a young photographer Linda was popular with up-and-coming pop groups. Her pictures of The Yardbirds, Otis Redding, Aretha Franklin, Cream, Jimi Hendrix, Stevie Winwood and, of course, The Beatles, began appearing in teen magazines such as *Sixteen* and *Hullaballoo* and then in *Life*.

'MY PHOTOGRAPHY IS VERY MUCH ABOUT GRABBING THE MOMENT.'

Linda met Paul McCartney in 1967 and married him two years later. She toured with *Wings* during the seventies as well as taking the cover photographs for the band's albums. But today most of Linda's photographs record the world of everyday people, her family, animals and the countryside. Although a natural photographer she is also keen on surrealism and says that she has been greatly influenced by Magritte. A vegetarian and outspoken campaigner for the conservation of the environment she believes that she can use her photography to move people, especially children, into an understanding of the suffering of wildlife in human hands.

'I DO PORTRAITS, I DO NATURE; I DO PEOPLE, AND ANIMALS, AND SURREALIST THINGS, AND OBSCURE THINGS. BUT IF I COULD, I WOULD CHOOSE AN ASSIGNMENT THAT WOULD CHANGE THE WORLD: SHOWING OUR CRUELTY TO ANIMALS AND ALSO THE HORROR AND CRUELTY OF MAN AGAINST MAN, AS IN WAR.'

Linda has published two books of her photographs, *Linda's Pictures* (1976) and *Photographs* (1982), and two calendars – one for the Council for the Protection of Rural England (1987) and another for the Wishing Well Appeal for Great Ormond Street Childrens' Hospital (1988). Her latest book *Sunprints* has just been published, a painterly portfolio of

Opposite: The Rye Art Gallery in the pretty Sussex town is one of the local galleries in which Linda McCartney exhibits her work, often featuring portraits of local people.

Interviewing Linda on camera over a cup of tea in the garden of the Rye Art Gallery. (Below.)

Linda's successful experiments in sun printing. This exposes light-sensitive chemically treated paper to light without need of a dark room or any form of processing.

> 'I GO THROUGH PERIODS OF GRAINY PHOTOGRAPHS — I LOVE GRAIN, IT'S KIND OF IMPRESSIONISTIC.'

For Linda McCartney the real thing is everything. She very rarely works in a studio, preferring to record images straight from nature. I went to meet Linda at the Rye Art Gallery to talk to her about her approach to photography. The opening picture in the gallery is a greatly enlarged portrait of a coal man. Linda was driving around with a 10 × 8 camera and simply responded to the craggy, characterful face of this man climbing down from his lorry.

The next picture we looked at, 'Boys on the beach', was also 'accidental'. One of Linda's favourites, it was taken twenty years ago on a Barbados seashore in low sunlight. It could not, she emphasises, be taken again. 'I'm not a particularly organised sort of person. I'm far more instinctive. I don't know how a particular photograph will come out.'

> 'I'M INTO NATURAL PEOPLE IN NATURAL LIGHT — I'VE NEVER BEEN A STUDIO PHOTOGRAPHER.'

Yet the pictures Linda took for the Council for the Protection of Rural England calendar, although naturalistic, are carefully considered. The grainy, impressionistic or even pointilist quality of the images were possible as much because of the high ASA film as natural conditions.

Linda McCartney lives close to nature

and has lately turned her attention to abstracts and sun prints, one of the simplest forms of photography and one with possibly the most 'accidental' results. Nonetheless, some of her portraits – such as the one of the artists Gilbert and George – seem as posed and as 'artificial' as the subjects. Perhaps this is just another example of Linda McCartney's empathy with the people and places she points her camera at.

SUSSEX COAL MAN. *This striking portrait
was blown up to a larger-than-life size for the
Rye Art Gallery exhibition. Such is the clarity
of the photograph that if you look hard Linda
can be seen reflected in the subject's coal-
black eyes. Like many of Linda's favourite
photographs the subject was found by
chance in the country lanes.*

BOYS ON THE BEACH. *One of Linda's personal favourites, this photograph was captured again by chance (or so she insists), as the sun began to drop on this West Indian beach, causing the figures to become what appear as perfectly posed silhouettes against the delicate wash of the sea.*

FIELD LANDSCAPE. *Linda's landscape photographs are remarkably natural images. An environmentalist, Linda is keen on recording the beauty of unspoilt landscapes and therefore promoting their preservation. There are no special tricks in a picture like this, only an eye for light and the choice of high speed film to capture the fine grain and texture of the landscape.*

ENGLISH SAND DUNES. *Linda believes in
travelling at all times of the day and night
in order to encounter interesting natural
conditions of weather and light, that bring out
the special qualities in her landscape pictures.
Here an ordinary English muddy beach is*

MIST OVER FIELDS. *'Just a typical mist near home' says Linda, describing this breathtaking photograph of an exhaling landscape. By getting to know a particular place intimately, whether a London suburb or a dale in Yorkshire, Linda believes that such opportunities will begin to present themselves to the familiar photographer. And no photographer could set up a shot like this.*

SILHOUETTE WITH CHURCH. *Amateurs
starting out are often advised not to get too
much sky in their viewfinders, yet the whole
point of this romantic portrait of a quintessen-
tial English rural landscape is the contrast
Linda has chosen to make between the depth
of the foreground and the shallowness of the
moody sky. The range of tone is very satisfying.*

SWANS IN MARSH. *Reminiscent of a pointillist painting, but unmistakably a Linda McCartney picture. This image was hand-tinted in a delicate wash of colours that enhance the subtle plays of light captured in the original black and white print. With hand-tinting and, more recently, her sun prints, Linda is constantly extending the range of her very natural approach to photography.*

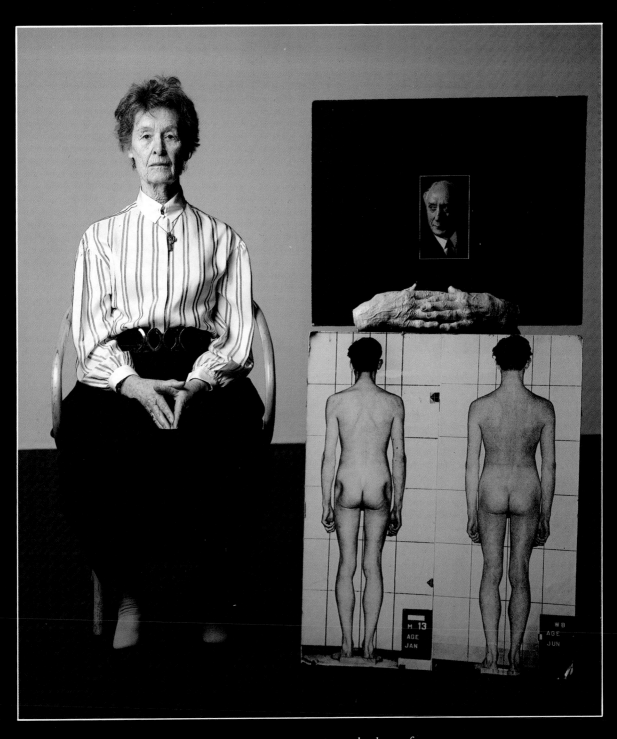

A SURREALIST MONTAGE *on the theme of
the Alexander technique, the innovative system
of body alignment. Linda's teacher sits facing
the camera; alongside her are 'before and after'
photographs of the back of a client, and a
portrait of Mr Alexander who developed the
technique. The preserved hands belong to him.*

Terence Pepper

Sue Davies

Chapter Six

For Love or Money?

Collecting for pleasure or investment – the value
of photography today in museums and marketplace.

John Kobal

Philippe Garner

It is difficult to know exactly how history will view the work of Heather Angel, the Duke of York, Terence Donovan, David A. Bailey, Albert Watson and all the other photographers I have talked to over the past year. How valuable is a photograph? Which is more valuable, a signed print by Norman Parkinson or the original negative he printed from? Do collectors and museums view photography as an art form or simply as a way of remembering the past? So, the next people I wanted to meet were the collectors, gallery owners and museum directors. What criteria do they apply for choosing one photographer's work or particular print over another? I talked to Terence Pepper of the National Portrait Gallery, Sue Davies and Zelda Cheatle of the Photographer's Gallery in London, John Kobal, the Canadian collector of historic Hollywood photographs, and Philippe Garner of Sotheby's, the London auction house.

PHOTOGRAPHS AS HERITAGE: THE NATIONAL PORTRAIT GALLERY

Terence Pepper has the job of advising curators at the National Portrait Gallery on period photography. Although photography was not on display in the National Portrait Gallery until as late as 1972, Terence explained that the gallery has been collecting photographs since it was set up in 1856.

Photography was first seen by the National Portrait Gallery as an instrument of record, and was not compared to a portrait in watercolour or oils. There is little doubt that public attitudes have changed in recent years, yet the gallery still persists in having only a very few photographs on display.

I was fascinated to come across a magnificent print depicting Captain Robert Scott, better known as Scott of the Antarctic, taken in 1911, the year before he and the other members of his expedition froze to death after they had failed to beat the Norwegian explorer Admunsen to the South Pole. The photograph, taken by Herbert Ponting, is undoubtedly, as Terence Pepper describes it, one of the great pictures of the Edwardian era. In many ways this is the definitive image we have of Scott, not least because we see him writing his famous diary: the one that recorded Captain Oates leaving the tent to die without encumbering his colleagues with those immortal words 'I am going out and may be some time', and Scott's own frostbitten scrawl on the last page 'I do not think I can write more. For God's sake look after our people.' In this moving photograph we see Scott at work with a wealth of personal and period detail surrounding him. There are leather cases with labels attached and photographs of Scott's wife holding the future

naturalist Peter Scott in her arms. 'A painter would never have caught such detail', says Terence. It may not have seemed so significant then, but it does now.

'WE HAVE PROBABLY OVER A HUNDRED THOUSAND IMAGES, INCLUDING A LOT OF ORIGINAL NEGATIVES, WHICH ARE YET TO BE PRINTED UP.'

However, this superb image is tucked away in an almost hidden corner. You need to bend down to see it properly. This does show that painting is still the dominant medium in the gallery. Paintings are certainly rarer than photographs. The National Portrait Gallery owns about five thousand paintings, but over one hundred thousand photographs and negatives.

'SOME PICTURES ALWAYS STAY UP, BUT OTHERS WE TRY TO CHANGE SO THAT IF THE PUBLIC COME IN FREQUENTLY THERE'S DIFFERENT THINGS TO SEE.'

Paintings also take precedence when it comes to new acquisitions. 'If a Van Dyck comes on to the market', Terence suggested, 'then it is highly likely that

the gallery would put in a bid and if successful this would eat up more than its total acquisition budget for the year. There would simply be nothing left to spend on photography.' Nevertheless the gallery does continue to collect and photographers with a sense of history do come and show their portfolios. There is, in fact, an opportunity for contemporary photographers to have their work displayed. I was fortunate enough to have my portrait of the present Duke and Duchess of York in the gallery because Terence thought it was the 'definitive shot'. It will be replaced when Terence finds a better one. But if you want to donate a portrait to the National Portrait Gallery it cannot be one of the local greengrocer or Aunty Dot at Blackpool. The gallery only collects photographs of people of national importance. Even so it has gathered, one way or another, a fascinating collection of antique prints, including gems like the daybook of the French photographer Camille Silvy who took over ten thousand portraits between 1860 and 1868, the years he ran a studio on London's Bayswater Road. 'Silvy's daybooks are a wonderful record of mid-Victorian costume and portraiture', says Terence.

When the gallery does display a photograph it tries to find what Terence has described as the 'definitive image'. These in their turn become the ones used in postcards and book illustrations. You will always see the same picture of Oscar Wilde taken by Napoleon Sarony on Wilde's tour of the United States in 1882. Yet, looking at the famous image in the National Portrait Gallery archives, Terence reminds me that this was just one of twenty pictures that Sarony took at the time. According to the gallery, the definitive picture of the Beatles taken at the height of Beatlemania in 1964 was

Opposite: Terence Pepper and me beside the portraits of the present Royal Family. Note my own photograph of HRH Prince Andrew and Sarah Ferguson!

One of a famous set of studio portraits (left) taken by Napoleon Sarony of the young Oscar Wilde on his 1882 tour of the United States.

The famous photograph of Captain Robert Falcon Scott (above) writing in his diary in the Antarctic, taken by Herbert Ponting in 1911.

A page from the album (below) of Camille Silvy, who ran a photographer's studio in London in the 1860s. It is a fascinating record of period dress and style.

A portrait of Sir Charles Wheatstone and family (below) taken by the photographer Antoine Claudet (1802-1875). A classic Victorian family group.

the one by Norman Parkinson. The Fab Four look a very jolly bunch in this well known photograph, but as Terence reveals, the next negative shows the Four scowling. So the gallery has the power to choose how to represent famous faces to the public.

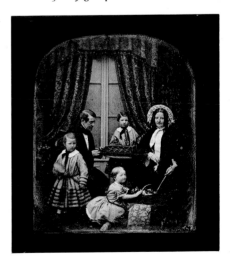

'USUALLY WE BUY THINGS TEN OR FIFTEEN YEARS AFTER THEY HAVE BEEN TAKEN. IT'S UNUSUAL TO GET SOMETHING CONTEMPORARY.'

We also look through photographs that have become valuable in my own lifetime but would never have been considered fit for a national collection when they were first taken. There is one of Cliff Richard and the Shadows on the set of 'Espresso Bongo' taken by the self-styled Father of Pop Photography, Harry Hammond, and another of Alma Cogan with Hammond reflected in the mirror. The gallery's latest acquisition, in keeping with their policy of collecting images of contemporary figures, is a portrait of boxer Frank Bruno with comedian Lenny Henry by Trevor Leighton.

But although the National Portrait Gallery does have a great collection of photographs, it is the paintings which are given pride of place. Looking at the image of Captain Scott I am not con-vinced. It would be nice to see a gallery given over exclusively to photography.

A very recent addition is this twin photograph of comedian Lenny Henry and boxer Frank Bruno, taken by Trevor Leighton.

PHOTOGRAPHS AS ART:
THE PHOTOGRAPHER'S GALLERY

Just up the road from the National Portrait Gallery is the Photographer's Gallery, a space given over to the display of contemporary work. The gallery was instituted by Sue Davies OBE, who previously worked at the ICA (Institute of Contemporary Arts) in London.

At the ICA, Sue was approached by many photographers, but at that time art galleries were largely uninterested. 'Art was getting very esoteric in the late sixties; it was art for a very particular audience who liked to be seen as an elite. Photography was obviously a popular art form and so looked down on.'

'NOW THAT THERE ARE LOTS OF OTHER MUSEUMS SHOWING PHOTOGRAPHY, A GREAT MEASURE OF OUR SUCCESS, WE ARE CONCENTRATING MORE ON CONTEMPORARY BRITISH PHOTOGRAPHERS AND THE INDEPENDENT SECTOR. THE 'HEROES' CAN NOW BE PUT ON AT THE BARBICAN AND HAYWARD.'

Sue set up the gallery in 1971 with the purpose of presenting new photographers to the public. 'There was nowhere else at the time. Fortunately, now, galleries such as the Barbican and the Hayward will show the work of major photographers, giving us the room to concentrate on fresh talent.' An informal gallery with no pretensions, the Photographer's Gallery receives about half a million visitors a year, including working photographers from all over the world who drop by to say hello to Sue

and her staff and perhaps to show their latest portfolios. Young photographers are always welcome to submit their work and gallery staff see about twelve new portfolios a week.

'MORE AND MORE PEOPLE ARE ENJOYING PHOTOGRAPHY AND REALISING THAT YOU CAN HAVE A PRINT ON THE WALL LIKE ANY OTHER FORM OF ART. IT IS A GROWING MARKET.'

During my visit I spoke to David Townend, a young photographer enjoying his first exhibition at the gallery. David's pictures show images of British public schools, a series of black and white images depicting boys in various settings. David found the gallery encouraging and helpful, but explains that although an exhibition like this is a good way to communicate a photographer's vision to a large public, there is no commercial incentive. 'Exhibiting here is not a question of hoping to impress people to get more work or to sell pictures, but to develop a rapport with the public.'

'CUSTOMERS CAN BE ANYONE FROM SOMEONE BUYING A PICTURE TO HANG ABOVE THEIR FIREPLACE TO A PURCHASER FROM A JAPANESE OR AMERICAN MUSEUM ADDING TO THEIR COLLECTIONS.'

But Zelda Cheatle, Print Room Manager at the Photographer's Gallery, does have the job of selling prints to the public as well as acquiring them for the gallery. Zelda holds the work of one hundred and fifty photographers. You

David Townend and me on the steps of the Photographer's Gallery off Leicester Square.

can visit at any time during the day and search through the files. You might be rubbing shoulders with a museum director buying in bulk as you look for a single image to hang in the hall.

'GALLERIES ARE GOOD FOR COMMUNICATING PHOTOGRAPHIC IDEAS TO PEOPLE WHO AREN'T NORMALLY INVOLVED IN PHOTOGRAPHY. THERE IS A TENDENCY FOR PEOPLE TO BE SCARED OF GALLERIES, BUT I HOPE THAT IDEA IS BREAKING DOWN AS MORE PEOPLE BECOME INVOLVED.'

What should people be looking for when they come to buy at the Photographer's Gallery? First of all Zelda insists that nobody should come looking for an investment. The gallery likes to sell prints to people who will appreciate them. Nevertheless most people know enough to ask for an 'original print'. I asked Zelda how the gallery defines an original print. 'In a nutshell', Zelda replies, 'it is an interpretation of the negative made by the photographer or under his supervision and signed by him.' So should negatives be destroyed after a certain number of prints have been made? This would certainly push up the price of limited edition 'original' prints. But Zelda says that a negative should be kept, and over time different series of prints can be run off them. They will not, of course, be signed by the photographer and so will not be quite as valuable.

How should people begin to collect prints? Zelda believes that people should be encouraged to follow their own instincts. A lot of people begin by collecting popular images such as reportage photography. Others start by specialising in a subject area they particularly like, such as landscapes. The gallery has prints that range from five pounds to several thousand. A Fay Godwin landscape, for example, will cost between one hundred and one hundred and fifty pounds. A Man Ray print will cost many

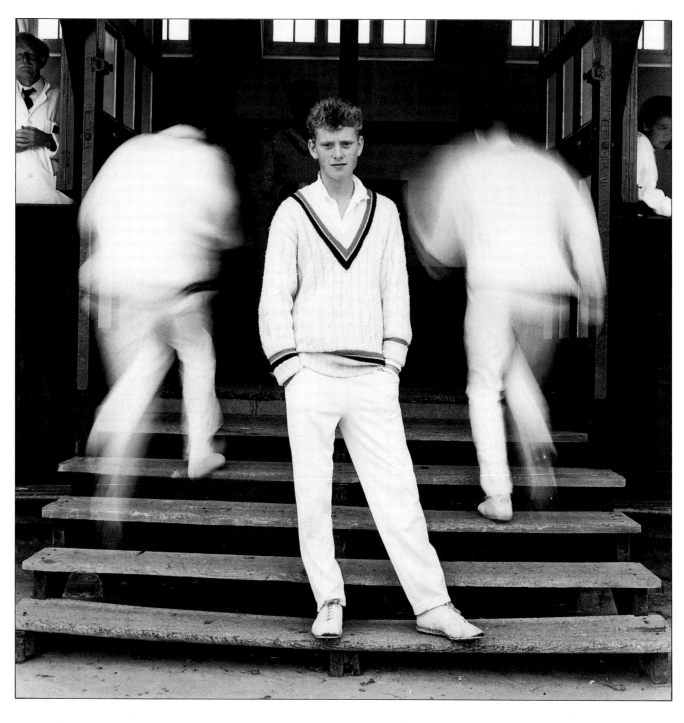

thousands. Zelda says that the market for contemporary prints is buoyant. 'There is such a great interest in photography that people come to the gallery; once here they find that there are prices to suit every pocket.' Sue Davies believes that people do need to be encouraged to buy more pictures than they do. 'I'm a great believer in moving pictures around in the house. I now have far more pictures than I have wall space at home, but if you keep the same pictures in the same places for years then they simply become a part of the furniture and you never really look at any of them.' By having a range of prints that are within the means of teenagers working in shops on Saturdays as well as museum directors, the Photographer's Gallery does encourage the public to buy photo-graphs. It may just be that some of these will turn out to be valuable, but this, Sue and Zelda believe, can only be by happy accident and not design.

David Townend's exhibition on the theme of public school included these views of a would-be England captain (opposite) and a matron (below). Both are a wonderful exercise in symmetry.

PHOTOGRAPHS AS OBJECTS OF BEAUTY: THE KOBAL COLLECTION

John Kobal owns one of the most popular collections of photographs to be found anywhere. For many years John, a Canadian living in London, has been collecting photographs of the American cinema and Hollywood stars. What began as a hobby has now become a way of life.

Many years ago, John was appalled to see historically important, beautifully crafted and lovingly shot prints of pre-war Hollywood being confined to the dust-bin. When you look at examples from John's superb collection you can hardly believe that anyone would throw away what have turned out to be some of the classic images of their genre. John has devoted years to seeking out the photo-graphers and studios, who were often quite happy to turn over to his care negatives and prints that they no longer wanted. We should all be grateful to John Kobal for saving many of the finest photographic images of Hollywood.

> 'THESE PHOTOGRAPHS ARE ART — YOU CAN SEE THE THOUGHT, THE PERCEPTIONS THAT WENT INTO THEM. IF IT HADN'T BEEN FOR PEOPLE LIKE ME, NONE OF THEM WOULD HAVE BEEN SAVED FOR US TODAY.'

John's decision to collect Hollywood photographs was an impulsive one at first and then a mission. Still, he has certainly been rewarded. His collection is now almost priceless. John explained that the price of a print depends not just on its age and subject matter, nor even on whether it is signed by the photo-

grapher. Assuming the image is one we value, sometimes the quality of the photographic paper is all-important. John pointed out how the range and quality of photographic paper has de-clined over the years. Look back through your family scrapbooks and you will see that this is true. 'We're talking about the difference between silk and nylon', says John emphatically. The new generation of high-speed colour printers produces an image from your exposed film yet does little justice to the richness inherent in many of your best negatives. The paper is not matched to the range of your images, while the printing process is too hurried to bring out any of the subtleties of light, shade and mood. Too many people either seem to accept these standards or else assume that either their camera or their ability to use it is at fault.

> 'I THINK I AM A GOOD COLLECTOR — I HAVE AN INSTINCT FOR IT. IF I LOST EVERYTHING TODAY, I'D JUST START COLLECTING AGAIN, BECAUSE THAT'S WHAT I'M GOOD AT. I'M GOOD AT SNIFFING THINGS OUT, LIKE TRUFFLE HOUNDS. AND, OF COURSE, BECAUSE I LIKE MOVIES SO MUCH.'

John owns many magnificent por-traits, finely crafted, of the legendary

Hollywood stars, from Greta Garbo and Clark Gable to Marilyn Monroe, Marlon Brando and Clint Eastwood. 'Some of the great actresses had photographers who followed in their footsteps for years. The best pictures of Katherine Hepburn, who loved having her picture taken, were the work of Ernest Bachrach, who shot almost all of her portraits during her first seven years in films. In these pictures, John says, Hepburn simply melts into the lens, emerging from the prints with a brand of vitality and charm that another photographer might have failed to capture.

> 'PHOTOGRAPHS ARE SOMETHING YOU CAN HOLD IN YOUR HAND, THAT YOU CAN FEEL ARE YOURS. THEY LINK ME TO THE MOVIE STARS I LOVE SO MUCH.'

Bette Davis apparently hated having her picture taken until she found the right photographer to transform what she thought were her defects into images that caught her fascinating personality and style. Greta Garbo, completely re-laxed in the company of a photographer she respected, appeared in front of the camera as she actually was: no make-up, freckles, wrinkles and a little scar on her brow. She trusted her photographer and the immense skill of his dramatic light-

> 'MY COLLECTION IS UNIQUE. IT RANGES ACROSS THE WHOLE HISTORY OF THE CINEMA, AND THE QUALITY IS VERY, VERY GOOD.'

ing, while he trusted what John refers to as 'a small army of retouchers' to produce the images of the divine Garbo

Opposite: With John Kobal outside his Hollywood Collection. John has saved thousands of now priceless Hollywood prints and negatives from the dustbin.

Marlon Brando (below left) portrayed in his early days (1951) by John Engstead. Brando was not always an easy sitter, and portraits of him soon became scarce. But for John Kobal, this photograph would now be as elusive as its enigmatic subject.

Joan Crawford (below right), according to John Kobal, loved being photographed. Her sultry character on and off screen is well caught in this dramatically shaded portrait by George Hurrell in 1933.

that film goers have admired for generations.

> 'THINK OF YOUR NEGATIVE AS THE 'SCORE' AND THE PRINTER AS THE 'CONDUCTOR' TO WHOM YOU ENTRUST YOUR COMPOSITION FOR ITS FIRST PERFORMANCE. THE VARIETY OF PHOTOGRAPHIC PAPERS A PRINTER CAN USE IS LIKE THE VARIETY OF AN ORCHESTRA: YOUR PRINT CAN BE AS MULTIPLE AND BLAND AS MUZAK, OR AS GRAND AND RICH AS THE EROICA.'

John's reports on the photographic treatment of individual stars are fascinating, but which of his pictures is the most valuable? Curiously it is not one of the stars, but a photograph made at the time of the cataclysmic earthquake that destroyed San Francisco in 1906. Taken on the spot by Arnold Genth, one of the most celebrated American photographers at the turn of the century, this vintage print is now considered priceless and would, at auction, fetch over ten thousand pounds. The photograph was a lucky find, yet John thinks you could be just as lucky with a little perseverance. 'Start by looking through the family albums; try the local junk shops. Even

with thousands of photo-buffs doing the same, you could still be lucky.' But in the end the importance of a photograph lies in the image and its printing, on whether it strikes a chord in the people who look at it. It will be a sad day when collectors begin locking photographic prints in bank vaults like Old Master paintings rather than having them on display.

A lovely essay in light and shade, this
glamorous portrait of Jean Harlow by George
Hurrell was taken to promote her film
'Reckless', and so is full of smouldering
sexuality. The lighting is luxurious, three-
dimensional and dramatic.

One of John Kobal's favourite Hollywood
photographs, this is a portrait of the silent film
star Louise Brooks, taken by Eugene R Richie.
In a superb piece of graphic design the
photographer's lights have blacked out
everything except the actress's profile, hands
and long pearl necklace. A picture that
captures the twenties.

PHOTOGRAPHS AS INVESTMENT: SOTHEBY'S AUCTION ROOMS

There is no getting away from the fact that historic photographs are becoming valuable and that an increasing number of collectors see them as a financial investment. To find out the sort of prices collectors are willing to pay, I went to see Philippe Garner, who is in charge of photography at Sotheby's the well-known London auctioneers.

Sotheby's has been holding photographic auctions since December 1971, marking, as Philippe says, 'the beginnings of the photographic market as we know it today'. 'It coincided', according to Philippe, 'with the development of sales in nineteenth-century art and applied arts. As photography is one of the great inventions of the Victorian era it seemed logical to focus on it as a subject for collectors.' Auction room sales had been held sporadically in the past elsewhere. In fact there have been auctions of collections since the earliest days of photography, certainly since the 1850s. The big change since then has been the frequency of such auctions and the tremendous prices that photographs now command.

'SOTHEBY'S IS DIFFERENT FROM A GALLERY IN THAT IT DOESN'T FORCE A PRICE FOR A PHOTOGRAPH.'

The British record to date for a photograph goes to an original of the famous print of the great Victorian engineer Isambard Kingdom Brunel standing against the launching chains of *The Leviathan* steamship (later renamed as *The Great Eastern*). That print sold for twenty thousand pounds. However, if you happen to have a copy of the Brunel print, don't get too excited. The day I visited Sotheby's there happened to be another Brunel print coming up for auction. This one, not in such good condition, was expected to make a mere three thousand pounds.

'I WAS THRILLED TO SEE A PHOTOGRAPH MAKE A THOUSAND POUNDS FOR THE FIRST TIME, MANY YEARS AGO. I REMEMBER PREDICTING THAT ONE DAY WE WOULD SEE A PHOTOGRAPH MAKE *FIVE* THOUSAND POUNDS – WHICH HAS NOW BEEN AND GONE. OUR PERSONAL RECORD AT SOTHEBY'S IS NOW TWENTY THOUSAND POUNDS.'

How are the prices set? This is Philippe's job, although as he is at pains to point out, Sotheby's cannot make the price. It can only suggest a figure that collectors are likely to pay. Philippe sets reserve prices according to precedent or through his understanding of what is realistic. If bidders think otherwise then of course there will be no takers; if the estimates were constantly over the top then vendors would eventually desert the auction house and sell their collections through other channels.

'I ALWAYS FEEL THAT THE PRIME REASON FOR BUYING A PHOTOGRAPH SHOULD BE, IN FACT, A TRUE PASSION FOR THE SUBJECT MATTER.'

What makes a photograph valuable? Aside from its subject matter and the reputation of the photographer, the most valuable prints are ones that Sotheby's

label 'vintage'. A vintage print is one made very soon after a photograph was taken and most probably by the photographer. Many photographers go back to old negatives years after a particular shot was taken to reprint favourite or best-selling images, but although a later print might be an improvement both technically and aesthetically, Philippe insists that a vintage print will command the highest price.

'SOMETIMES WE MAY NOT APPRECIATE THE TRUE WORTH OF SOMETHING, AND IT MAKES TWENTY OR THIRTY TIMES OUR ESTIMATE. THIS HAS HAPPENED ONCE OR TWICE, AND IS ALWAYS THE SOURCE OF SURPRISE AND EXCITEMENT.'

What about fakes? Philippe is reassuring. 'Photographic papers of particular periods are incredibly difficult to reproduce, so the chances of failing to spot a fake are pretty slim.' On the day of my visit to Sotheby's there were no obvious fakes coming up for bidding. Instead there was a fascinating selection of

The highest price yet paid at Sotheby's for a photograph was £20,000 for a first-class print of this famous 1857 photograph of the Victorian engineer Isambard Kingdom Brunel. Other prints of the same photograph may sell for only £2000 — it all depends on often marginal differences of quality.

historic prints, ranging from the lesser Brunel print already mentioned, a photograph by Charles Dodgson (better known as Lewis Carroll, author of *Alice in Wonderland*) through to 'vintage' copies of Bill Brandt's 'Year on the beach' and 'Girl in a London room'. The Brandts were expected to make between five hundred and nine hundred pounds each, a good deal less than a book entitled *Life and Landscape in the Norfolk Broads* by the distinguished Victorian photographer Emerson, the star of the show, which Philippe estimated at ten thousand pounds.

'A BUYER IS OFTEN CONCERNED THAT HE BIDS FOR A PRINT THAT IS RARE OR THE ONLY ONE AVAILABLE. IF MORE PRINTS OF EQUAL QUALITY TURN UP, THEIR VALUE IS UNDERMINED. HOWEVER THE MARKET HAS BEEN ESTABLISHED LONG ENOUGH NOW FOR US TO HAVE DEVELOPED A PRETTY GOOD FEEL AS TO THE RELATIVE RARITIES OF PARTICULAR PHOTOGRAPHS.'

Even though prices seem to have gone through the roof, there are still plenty of historic photographs available at around the fifty to one hundred pound mark. Most will rise in value, but Philippe hopes that people are collecting for the pleasure photographs give them rather than for pure profit.

Philippe, by the way, has some advice for those thinking of starting a collection of historic photographs. 'If you come to an auction for the first time, sit on your hands and don't bid for anything. Just watch what goes on. Then spend some money on a good set of reference books,

go to a lot of exhibitions and galleries, get a feel of what you want and how the selling process works. And then come back and bid.' Or maybe come back and sell. Who knows what priceless prints might be lurking in those old family albums?

INDEX

ACKNOWLEDGEMENTS

THE PUBLISHERS AND GENE NOCON would like to thank the following for their contributions to the book: Richard Young, Terry O'Neill, Albert Watson, David A. Bailey, HRH the Duke of York, Heather Angel FRPS, Terence Donovan, Linda McCartney, Terence Pepper, John Kobal, Sue Davies OBE, Zelda Cheatle and Philippe Garner. Also the *Daily Express*, Ross Benson, Terry Evans, Peter Stringfellow, Stephanie Powers, Dolph Lundgren, Jane Seymour, Michael Caine, Pam Ross, *Vogue* Magazine, Virgin Airways, Rexford Darko, Barry Robinson and The Post Office, Cara Young, the Tottenham Camera Club and David Townend.

THE PUBLISHERS would also like to thank the following for their help with providing certain photographs: The Photographer's Workshop, Rex Features, Camera Press, The Post Office, Harrison's the Printers, Barbara Heller Photo Library, Biofotos, The Rye Art Gallery, The National Portrait Gallery, The Photographer's Gallery, The Kobal Collection and Sotheby's.

They would also like to thank Mike Wade for design, Chris Branfield for paste-up and Alex Corrin for indexing.

GENE NOCON would like to thank David Mason and the Thames Television production crew, Joanna Lorenz, Jonathan Glancey, Ann-Louise, Chris, Nick and Henry, and everyone involved with the television series and the book. Without their help none of this would have been possible. Many thanks!

THE THAMES TELEVISION SERIES *Nocon on Photography* was written and produced by David Mason. David joined Thames in 1977, writing and appearing in the children's comedy series 'You must be Joking'. He then wrote the documentary 'the DC3' before working for six years with Eamonn Andrews on 'This is your Life'. It was through this programme that David met Gene Nocon and developed the idea for a special series on photography.

The Thames Television production team included Annette Clark (Researcher), John Tagholm (Executive Producer), Chris Bould (Director) and Alison Eisbury (Production Assistant).

JONATHAN GLANCEY, a Fellow of the Royal Society of Arts, has edited and written for many publications, including *Tatler*, *Blueprint*, The Architectural Press and *Architectural Review*. He is publishing director of the Design Analysis International group, and has recently been appointed design correspondent of the *Independent*.

Cover photographs: the front cover portraits were taken by Gene Nocon except for picture of Linda McCartney by Graham Hughes. The portrait of Gene on the back flap is by Mrs Kathleen Ford and the photograph on the back cover is by Albert Watson.